Londonderry Farewell

Londonderry Farewell

An Untold Story

Captain Tom McKeown USN
John Fraim

GreatHouse Stories

Registered Writers Guild of America West
No. 1687767

ISBN: 1542932998
ISBN 13: 9781542932998
Library of Congress Control Number: 2017901896
CreateSpace Independent Publishing Platform
North Charleston, South Carolina

Disclaimer

This book is historical fiction. It reflects the author's present recollections of experiences over time. Some names and characteristics have been changed, some events have been added or compressed, and some dialogue has been recreated.

To

Mary E. McKeown
1931–2015

and

Martha Fraim
1920–2013

The Town I Loved So Well
Phil Coulter

In my memory, I will always see
The town that I have loved so well
Where our school played ball by the gas yard wall
And they laughed through the smoke and the smell
Going home in the rain, running up the dark lane
Past the jail, and down behind the Fountain
Those were happy days in so many, many ways
In the town I loved so well

Now the music's gone but they carry on
For their spirit's been bruised, never broken
They will not forget but their hearts are set
On tomorrow and peace once again
For what's done is done and what's won is won
And what's lost is lost and gone forever
I can only pray for a bright, brand-new day
In the town I love so well

Derry Orchestra at Guild Hall

Contents

Acknowledgments

Former military and civilian personnel of the
US Navy base and naval communication station,
Londonderry, Northern Ireland

NAVCOMMSTA Londonderry Alumni Association

The residents of Londonderry, Northern Ireland

Sean McLaughlin (the *Derry Journal*)

Patrick Byrne for his relentless encouragement

Palm Springs Writers Guild for their guidance

Diane Church for editing and support

Prologue

Very little has been written about the "troubles" in Northern Ireland. Yes, we saw headlines and articles in the press when incidents took place. But not much is told about the people and their feelings or the long-term effects this time had on their lives. This is a special story of intrigue, terror, fear, and sadness brought about by the forced closing of one of the most important, earliest US naval bases in Europe and the tearful farewell by sailors and their families to the town they loved so well—a love developed from thirty-five years of living and working together on a navy base amid the political strife in Northern Ireland.

The Irish are a very proud people with a great sense of humor. It's difficult for all of us to imagine the terror and brutality that permeated the land in those darkest days. Yet, the humor and laughter never went away. This city of winding walls is a beautiful city today. It is peaceful and one of the most attractive places to visit in Europe. This story is long overdue. It is about a love affair that grew deeper every year, through thick and thin. And no matter what, that love still exists today—laughing, crying, and marrying. Starting in 1943 and ending in 1977, American sailors spent their paychecks throughout the town of Londonderry—in pubs, shops, homes, restaurants, and churches and on golf courses, riding trails, fishing holes, and dance halls. At least one sailor was always mingling with the locals. Catholics and Protestants, Nationals and Unionists shared the facilities and festivities on the US naval base. At the time of its closing in 1977, it was the oldest US naval facility in Europe.

We must apologize to the city, its people, and the Derry sailors for taking so long to write this story. Granted, there were some happenings that were classified by the US government especially as they related to the "troubles." But the underlying point of the story is to explain the unique and endearing relationship between the people of Londonderry and the US Navy. It tells how the Americans were able to escape the terrorist conflicts because of their Derry friendships, despite the deeply distorted religious and political factions.

Always in the background of this story is the suspense and emotional stress of secretly turning over the oldest naval base in Europe to the British Army, a very surprising and unpopular event for both sides of the warring religious parties. More history can be found in "The Beginnings" (appendix 2).

The city of Londonderry itself is the real heroine of this story. We have tried to portray her courage, her music, her picturesque beauty, and her friendly people. It is a legacy of love that still remains to this day between the city and all the Americans who were privileged to serve at the US Navy base in Londonderry, Northern Ireland.

This is a historical novel that attempts to provide an honest blend of fact and fiction. In most cases, fictional names are used to describe persons; in other areas, such as places and things, the reader is entitled to know when there is a difference. It is not the author's purpose to place blame on any religious or social faction or political party for the despicable "troubles".

Introduction

In the spring of 1976, a young navy captain, Tom McKeown, was called into the office of one of the top admirals at the Pentagon and told his assignment was to close the US Naval Communications Station in Londonderry, Northern Ireland, and simultaneously expand the Naval Communications Station in Thurso, Scotland. Captain McKeown, under personal pressure but with the support of his family and his naval personnel, carried out this assignment.

Originally, Captain McKeown had little more than memories and some souvenirs to begin his reconstruction effort of events that happened thirty-five years ago. There were several faded photographs, an old box of slides, and a few pages of typed notes. It wasn't much.

But there was also the memory of the incredible time Captain McKeown spent in Northern Ireland, and this kept him pushing forward to complete this story. As it turns out, the captain was not the only one who maintains memories of an untold story of Londonderry and the navy communications station. Over the years, there has developed a group called the US NAVCOMMSTA Londonderry Alumni Association, and they maintain, to this day, an extensive website and sponsor annual alumni gatherings.

Captain McKeown reached out to members of the alumni association who served on the base prior to or during the time he was commanding officer. He also made contact with the people of Londonderry. The response was tremendous and far greater than he could ever imagine. In this way, something that began as the memoir of one man has become a collective memory of so many who lived, loved, and experienced a particular place and time.

Chapter 1

A Sailor's Dream, Home with Family

A Little League baseball game was in progress at a park in Washington, DC. It was a week after the huge bicentennial Fourth of July celebration, and the city was still cleaning up. Red, white, and blue banners lined the perimeter of the field, but there were some volunteers on ladders beginning to take them down. Patriotic flyers were still being cleaned up from the streets. The event was over, but the city was still filled with patriotic pride. It was the top of the ninth inning with two outs, and the Springfield Dragons were tied 10 to 10 with the Columbia Heights Tigers. I was the coach of the Springfield Dragons. I am in my mid 40's, about five foot ten, slim, with wavy black hair (closely trimmed to meet navy regulations). I knew my blue eyes were twinkling with pride, and my face, tan from many days at sea, was glowing in the late sun. I paced back and forth on the sidelines near third base in my "Spirit of 76" T-shirt, shouting instructions to my son, Shawn, who danced around third base, ready to make the winning run at home plate—just sixty feet away.

"Watch the pitcher, Shawn," I shouted. "Make your move when he's committed and not before."

Shawn looked at me briefly and shook his head. He had learned over the years that he could take the advice of his father to the bank. Shawn knew I was not a man who liked to lose at anything.

The fourteen-year-old boy with long blond hair closely watched the pitcher and made his move right after the batter hit the ball. No time to see the results of the hit. Shawn took off toward home plate. The ball was a grounder to the short stop, who scooped it up and fired toward home plate, just as Shawn slid over it.

"Safe!" declared the umpire, and the game was over.

The Springfield Dragons surrounded Shawn, who was getting up from home plate while shaking dust off his pants. I smiled. I was so proud of my son. It was great to be home and be a part of the family again.

"Great coaching," said one of the fathers to me. "How long are you back for?"

"A long time," I replied. "I can feel it this time."

"You ever consider coaching soccer in the fall?" the other father asked.

"Why not?" I said. "My daughter, Colleen, loves soccer."

On the ride back home, I praised Shawn and told him how proud I was of him.

"You watched the pitcher just like I told you to."

"I just wish you were around more," Shawn said.

"I know. This time, it's different. I'm back for a long time. I can feel it."

"I'm glad," Shawn replied.

Half an hour later, Shawn and I arrived at a small ranch-style home in Springfield, Virginia. It was on a street with a lot of other similar-style ranch homes. I had just bought the home for my family, and a number of projects were in various stages of completion. There was the smell of fresh paint throughout the home. A large book of wallpaper samples sat on the kitchen table. Chips of painting colors were Scotch-taped to the walls.

My wife, Mary, was busy measuring various spaces in the home with a tape measure. She showed me a collection of carpet samples.

"I think this dark beige is great for the living room," she said, pushing a sample in front of me.

"It looks great," I replied.

Over the years, I had learned that there was not much to be gained by not agreeing with her. And besides, she seemed so happy. But our homes had always been such temporary affairs.

It was late afternoon, and the eastern sun was sitting on the roof of the little ranch house. In the backyard, the barbecue was glowing. I had some hamburgers grilling, and my six-year-old daughter, Tara, and thirteen-year-old daughter, Colleen, were begging for a hamburger.

Tara came up to me, holding her stuffed hobbit that I had given her. Her first-grade class had been reading about hobbits. It had since become almost like another appendage to Tara, as she was seldom without it.

"Can you get me a real hobbit someday?" she asked.

"We'll see, but you know hobbits are very nasty and very difficult to catch."

We enjoyed our burgers around the new picnic table we had just purchased. Tara sat next to me with her hobbit sitting on the picnic bench next to her. The kids were talkative, telling me about their school year, which I had missed.

Meanwhile, Mary handed me a brochure.

"What's this?"

"Hawaii," Mary said. "I've always wanted to go there."

I looked through the brochure while munching on my hamburger and chatting with the children.

"I thought we could plan to spend this Christmas in Hawaii," Mary said quietly. "It'd be great to get out of the cold winter weather here in Virginia."

"Not a bad idea. We could visit the navy base over there."

"Why don't you ever get assigned to places like Hawaii?" Mary asked.

I laughed. "That would be something."

"Are there hobbits in Hawaii?" Tara asked.

"No," I replied. "Hobbits come from Middle Earth."

"But I want to go to Hawaii, I want to go to Hawaii, I want to go to Hawaii!"

"Can we go to Hawaii?"

I picked Tara up and gave her a big hug.

"Maybe someday."

"You're not going away again are you, Dad?" Colleen asked. "I don't want you to go away."

"I'm staying home. I'm here for good."

Shawn, my 15-year-old little leaguer then asked Mary, "When are Tommy and Jimmy coming home?"

Mary replied, "Tommy is working in Maryland, and Jimmy is playing college baseball for Ferrum University. They both will be home in about two weeks."

When the children had gone to bed, Mary and I enjoyed a quiet moment alone.

Mary lifted a glass of wine. "So good to have you back," she said. "I hope it's for good."

"Me too. In the meantime, I will plan a trip to Hawaii."

Her lovely smile and her green eyes twinkled in the dark of the night, and her beautiful blond hair shone in the moonlight. I'm a lucky guy. We toasted, and I kissed her cheek.

Chapter 2

Pentagon Meeting

I pulled files out of a box and put them into a filing cabinet. Just like the new home I was moving into, I was also moving into a new office at the Pentagon. I had been away for a year as commander of a navy destroyer in the Atlantic, and it was good to be home with the family and great to think that this might be home for a while.

I walked around my new office and looked at the photos I had just put on my walls. These early photos of the family were taken when I was an ensign and featured the various bases to which I was assigned; the photos of me alone depicted solo navy missions around the world together with my year as commanding officer of the base in the Republic of Vietnam; of a new LST (landing ship tank) out of Little Creek, Virginia; and of the USS *Leary* (DD-879).

Since graduating from Seton Hall University and receiving a master's in communications from the Naval Postgraduate School in Monterey, California, I had been on the naval fast track, gaining my stripes much faster than most. Now, at forty-four, I was a full four-stripe captain.

But there was an inner happiness that showed on my face. I had found a particular calling in life. Some men had a daily drudge. But always, I had a mission rather than a job. It had made all the difference to me. And somewhere, subconsciously, I wondered whether my family would win out over my career. Maybe it was this way with other men—those who had a family and also those who went it alone. What a strange demographic.

Three months later, when the files were all put into the filing cabinets, I sat down behind my huge desk. The image was such a contrast to all the photos on the walls. Looming over the space of the large desk, it seemed like the command center rising over the flight deck of an aircraft carrier. I began going through my daily, ubiquitous stack of papers overflowing from my inbox. I signed a few letters. I dictated some memos to my assistant, shuffled papers around, and put them into various piles. It seemed like I had been repeating this routine for way more than a few months. It had been a long time since I was behind a desk all day.

Suddenly, my office door opened, and a marine orderly entered, snapped to attention, and clicked his heels. In the manner of a drill sergeant, at full volume, he sounded off, "Sir, the admiral wants to see you immediately, sir. Right now, sir, immediately, sir."

I waved the marine away, telling him I would be on my way in a few minutes. But the marine insisted I go with him immediately. What a pain in the ass! I was perturbed at his attitude, but I followed him. We walked down the long, wide Corridor E of the Pentagon, past countless doors with names and military designations. I suffered a few brief assignments at the Pentagon over my career, but I had never liked the place. My real navy home had been those moving islands of steel in the middle of the ocean.

~~~

Finally, we arrived at Admiral Schmidt's office and walked past the desks of his assistants arranged outside his private office like escort ships around a great aircraft carrier. The marine orderly opened the door, and I walked into Admiral Schmidt's office. There were quite a few men assembled in the office: Robert Hunt from the office of the Secretary of the State Department, Ralph Douglas from the CIA, Peter Spencer from the Office of the Secretary of Defense (SECDEF), and Ian Radcliff from the British embassy.

Everyone was sitting around a long, polished mahogany conference table. There were no smiles, just disconcerted and grim-looking faces. I wondered what in the hell I had done wrong this time.

Admiral Schmidt, in his early fifties with a rather strong physique, entered the room, and all stood. "Good morning, gentlemen; please sit down." The admiral turned directly to me and expounded, "Tom, we have a serious matter on our hands, and we need you to carry out a critical mission. I am going to send you to Northern Ireland to take command of the naval base in Londonderry. The president himself wants us to close that base as soon as possible. It is in the middle of a dangerous religious conflict. The president is *hot* on this. Peter Spencer tells us that SECDEF is trying to reason with him, since our North Atlantic Fleet depends on Londonderry. However, gentlemen, a decision has been made, and we've got the ball. We must get all hands out of Derry safely, including women and children, without any incidents or conflict, and still support the fleet. Tom, I have asked you here because I need someone like you with your background and experience to do the job."

Ian Radcliff from the British embassy interjected, "Admiral, it should be made clear the navy base will be turned over to the British Army, which needs to expand in Northern Ireland in order to establish proper law and order and increase security checkpoints. I must point out, however, that neither the Loyalists nor the Catholics—and especially the Provisional IRA—want more of the British Army."

The admiral responded, "Now, look, all of you! This is a dangerous mission. If the IRA finds out we intend to turn it over to the British Army, there will be more threats and the people on the base will be put in mortal danger. This must be kept top secret." The admiral then turned to me. "Tom, what do you think?"

"Admiral, first of all, I'm an Irish Catholic. My ancestors will turn over in their graves to see me go into Northern Ireland, and, Admiral, I've only been home with my family for three months."

The admiral quickly responded, "Tom, you can take your family with you if you wish—although there is danger—and as far as being an Irish Catholic, that's one of the reasons I've selected you."

Furthest from my mind that day was any notion that I would be getting sudden orders to an overseas assignment, let alone Northern Ireland. Why in the world would the navy want to even think about moving me so soon? I just finished two back-to-back combat-related tours, first as commanding officer of a navy base in CanRahn Bay, Republic of Vietnam, where after a year, we turned over the base to South Vietnam, and then as commanding officer (CO) of a destroyer, the USS *Leary* DD-879, which I eventually turned over to the Spanish navy.

After nearly four years, it was great to be home with the family and to get to know my wife again. Then it came to me. I was a turnover expert. I was a closer. Just my luck!

The admiral continued, "Since World War II, we've had naval operations in Northern Ireland. As you might know, the facilities around Londonderry played a key role in the Battle of the Atlantic. After the war, many of the operations in the area were closed down, except for a communications station in Londonderry, which has been in continuous operation."

The admiral pushed a notebook across the table toward me.

"Tom, take a look," he said, "photos of the base through its history—our oldest naval base in Europe."

I looked at the photos in the notebook. There were black-and-white photos from the days of World War II and photos of young sailors lifting pints of Guinness in celebration of the end of the war. I also looked through the photos of technical base operations after the war through the late 1940s to the 1960s. There were photos of sailors in downtown Londonderry shopping, walking hand in hand with ladies, and visiting pubs, all smiling faces. It looked like a carefree time and a wonderful tour for the sailors.

Then, the photos in the notebook began to change. There were photos of tanks and troops in the streets of Londonderry and heavy barbed-wire fence around the navy base. There were photos of shootings and streets full of tanks and machine guns in the hazy mist of tear gas.

"As you can see," said Admiral Schmidt, "things began to change in Londonderry in the late sixties when religious and political matters in Northern Ireland exploded. It has been nearly two decades of turbulence and violence in Northern Ireland. Bloody, deadly conflicts and street battles erupted frequently between the passionately loyal Irish Protestants and the equally passionate and desperate Irish Catholics. Hand grenades were often thrown into pubs, killing all inside. Bloody Sunday in 1972, in the streets of Londonderry, was a horrible example of raw, inhumane conflict. British security forces, who intended to maintain order, were also in the line of fire. The president of the United States is deeply concerned that an American citizen will be killed, injured, or involved in the dreadful terrorist bombings and murders going on in Northern Ireland. After all, the British are our closest ally, as he often proclaims. He was shocked and outraged when told by the secretary of defense that there is a US Navy base in Northern Ireland and in Londonderry, the same site as Bloody Sunday."

The admiral waved his arm toward Robert Hunt from the State Department.

"The base still has strategic significance for our communications in the Baltic, North Atlantic, and Mediterranean. But the president wants us out of there," Hunt said. "He is concerned there will be an attack on the base and the nation will be pulled into conflict over there. He is worried how this could jeopardize our relationship with the British and the Republic of Ireland."

"The US Naval Communications Station (NAVCOMMSTA) is situated right in the middle of the so-called religious 'troubles' in Northern Ireland," said Peter Spencer from the Department of Defense. He pushed a few photos across the table toward me. The photos showed a mass of tangled metal. "The microwave tower on the base," Spencer said. "Bombed in seventy-three by the IRA. They were trying to blow up the supply building at the base and get to the armory but were not successful."

"But we know they will keep trying," said Ian Radcliff from the British embassy in London. He pushed a folder labeled "Classified" across the table to me. "A few years of correspondence between our embassy in London and Washington," he said. "We've been lucky so far, but intelligence tells us they'll keep trying."

"Besides the danger of the base being there," Admiral Schmidt added, "we can operate far more economically without out the added cost of additional security if we close the base at Londonderry and expand the navy communications facility at Thurso, Scotland. We have never publically revealed the Londonderry base, nor have we kept it a secret. Its mission is to support the Allied forces in the North Atlantic, especially the submarines. It is a very sensitive topic."

The admiral looked at me. "You're the man for this operation," he said. "You did a good job at CamRahn Bay, and then again turning over the USS *Leary* to Spain. We want you to take over from Captain Barker and see that the base is closed down without any violence. You need to keep the base in operation until our expanded base in Thurso, Scotland, is ready. Then, you'll be in charge of this base also. We can't just shut the Londonderry base down until the new communications station in Thurso is up and running."

"It's a very delicate and dangerous operation," said Ralph Douglas from the CIA. "We are turning the base over to the British Army. However, our public story is that the base is going back to the queen, and she will decide what to do with it and the property. It's critical we keep to this cover story. If the IRA ever finds out the ultimate fate of the base is to go the British Army, we are sure they will try to prevent this at all costs by sabotaging the base. A lot of American sailors and their families and Irish employees could be killed."

When Ralph Douglas was finished, there was a moment of silence around the table. I was beginning to realize why all the faces around the table were so grim.

The admiral addressed me. "Take a few days off to discuss all of this with your family. We need you there in three or four weeks to take over from Captain Barker. Family or not."

"Yes, sir," I said, standing up and saluting the admiral.

The admiral returned the salute, and everyone around the table stood up. After I left the admiral continued, "What do you think?"

"He is an Irish Catholic," said Robert Hunt from the State Department.

"He's more of a loyal navy man than a faithful Catholic," Admiral Schmidt responded.

"Maybe so," said Hunt. "But the base has always had a Protestant commanding officer. Thirty-five years and no Catholic commanding officer."

"With the troubles going on with the IRA, it's time for a Catholic to run the base," said Admiral Schmidt.

⌇

My head was swirling as I walked back to my office down the wide Corridor E. Mixed emotions banged against each other in my mind like bumper cars at an amusement park. In some ways, I longed to escape from my new prison behind the heavy wooden desk surrounded by photos from the past. But the Pentagon prison offered a home life. I had to weigh this need for home life against the challenge of command.

I wanted so much to be a husband and father again. I wanted to see my children grow and coach more baseball and soccer games. I had been away for so damn long—back and forth, coming in and out of the life of my family. Each time I saw a few more inches on the children and each time more of a look of weariness on Mary's face. But she seemed hopeful for the first time in a long while that I would be home and that we might be able to gain back some of those lost years, that we might be able to become somewhat of a normal family. But then I thought they would love visiting the Republic of Ireland on the holidays.

Taking part of the family with me to Ireland was dangerous, but it seemed that it was the only option to keep the family together. I would talk to Mary about it and tell her we had a chance to visit the place of our ancestry, a conversation we had had before. However, I wouldn't tell her about the dangers involved. She would never go with me, and the marriage would be over. I was certain of that.

Chapter 3

Family Dilemma

Ocean City, Maryland, was a popular resort town on the Atlantic coast 150 miles southeast of Washington, DC. The town was at the southern end of a long, narrow peninsula that was a summer playground for many Washingtonians.

It was early evening, and the last light of the western sun made a few final reflections in the Atlantic. Mary and I had driven over there for an evening together. The children had been farmed out to friends for the night. We were seated at a romantic table in a restaurant on the beach. A candle in a jar between us danced about from the mild breeze coming through the open windows. Two glasses of Chianti wine and a plate of cheese sat next to the candle. Over everything, we could hear the background music of the popular song, "In the Still of the Night," being so emotionally done by Frank Sinatra. It was hard to escape. I had often sung it to myself while standing on the wing of the bridge gazing at the moon and stars, especially the words, "Do you still love me as I love you?"

"So what is this big surprise you've been telling me about?" Mary asked.

"You know how we've talked about going to Ireland."

"You're taking us on a vacation to Ireland!" Mary replied.

"Better than a vacation," I said, pulling out a small map of Northern Ireland and putting it on the table near the light of the candle. "There's a base in Londonderry the navy is closing down, the oldest navy base in Europe. They want me to be the commanding officer of the base to manage the base closure."

"You told them no of course."

"It wasn't my prerogative to say yes or no."

"I can't believe you. You've been home for three months. We just bought a new house. The kids are excited to have you home. For the first time, I can see some stability in our life. And you're leaving all this to go to Ireland?"

"I want the family to go with me. You know you've always wanted to go to Ireland. We can both explore family roots."

Mary fumbled with the map on the table for a few seconds without saying anything.

"The kids are getting settled in the new school system, and I've made some new friends on our street."

"It won't be a long command. Nine months—a year at the max. It'll be a great experience for the children."

Mary took a sip of wine and looked absently out over the sand at the darkening Atlantic.

"Aren't there some problems in Northern Ireland?" Mary asked. "I've heard about the IRA and bombings."

"The problems over there are highly exaggerated. Besides, they all love the Americans, and what could be safer than a navy base?"

Mary didn't seem to hear what I was saying. I could see that her eyes were watering, and soon, a tear slowly rolled down her cheek.

"I was looking forward so much to our new life together—your new position at the Pentagon, you being home with the family, and us getting to know each other again."

"We'll just transfer our life to Ireland for a little while."

Hearing this, Mary abruptly got up from the table, spilling her wine. "I'm going back to the room," she announced. "I need to be alone right now. I've been alone so much, maybe we should just separate."

I watched her go and sat alone at the table, the candle in the bottle dancing around as I finished off the bottle of Chianti. I bought another bottle of Chianti and walked out over the wide beach of Ocean City. I sat down on the wet sand with my bottle, while the waves kept rolling in close to my feet.

Lights twinkled north up the shore like a long electric necklace. I sat in the sand and drank from the bottle of wine, looking out over the Atlantic Ocean, trying to see the future somewhere out there.

Then, I noticed the running lights of a ship on the horizon and recalled the many lonely nights I spent on the sea. Yes, I loved the sea, but I loved my family more.

Around two o'clock in the morning, I pulled myself together and headed back to the hotel room. Hoping that Mary was asleep, I undressed and staggered into bed.

"Where the hell have you been?" she asked.

"I've been sitting on the beach, thinking how beautiful you are and how much I love you."

Mary stared into my eyes and replied, "I love you too. Don't forget I invented 'the penny throwing game'. You know when I saved pennies while you were out to sea; then threw them on the front lawn for the kids to find when you came home, so you and I could run upstairs to bed while they were out of the house."

"I guess we will accompany you to Northern Ireland. We should tell the kids and put the house up for rent. I don't want to sell it! How much time do we have before we need to leave?"

"We have three or four weeks, but all we need to take with us is ourselves and our clothing. The house we will rent furnished, as our quarters in Ireland will be move-in ready and we will have a full-time maid."

Mary stared at me and merely shook her head.

"I'm sorry all the children will not be going with us as Jimmy will be in college and Tommy had just started a new business" I mentioned.

"Well, Jimmy is OK because he lives in the dorm, but I worry about Tommy—his new business and unstable living conditions. Do you think Tommy will be OK here by himself?"

"Yes, I think he'll be OK, and I'll have him visit us often."

"So we're only taking Shawn, Colleen, and Tara? Breaking up the family for your career?"

"Look, honey, I have no choice; I must go, and I don't want us to be separated anymore."

Chapter 4

Arrival in Ireland

I opened my eyes and pushed up the shade on the navy plane to look out the window at the Atlantic Ocean. I looked at my watch. It was three in the afternoon, and we had been in the air for six hours and should be getting close to Ireland. I unbuckled my seat belt and gently moved Mary's head from my shoulder, where she had been sleeping for a few hours. The rest of the family was asleep across the aisle. Tara had her hobbit next to her, strapped into a seat. Colleen was wearing the green T-shirt with "Ireland" on it, and Shawn was sleeping with his head against the window, wearing his trademark reverse New York Yankees baseball cap.

There were a few other navy personnel on the plane, and they were also sleeping. I made my way up the aisle toward the pilots in the cockpit.

"How far out are we?" I asked, leaning forward between the two pilots.

"Just half an hour from land, Captain," said the pilot. "You can see the island coming up now."

I looked out the cockpit window, and there it was. In the midafternoon sun from the west, the island glowed and waved with a supernatural color of green I had never seen before.

"It's beautiful!" I exclaimed.

"Of course it is," said the pilot. "It's Ireland."

There was a tap on my shoulder, and I turned around to see Mary standing behind me.

"Just woke up," she said. "How far are we?"

I pointed to the incredible sight in front of the plane as I moved aside for Mary to see out the cockpit window.

"Not far," I said.

"Oh my God, it's so beautiful," Mary said. "Forty shades of green," she whispered. "Do you remember my dad telling us that?" She squeezed my shoulder.

Half an hour later, we were over the spectacular green patchwork of Ireland, each parcel a different size and color, bordered by stone and hedges. The plane began descending for our landing in Shannon, Ireland. The family was awake, and everybody was looking out the window. The children were excited. And there was even a slight hint of excitement on Mary's face. It had taken a lot of convincing to get her to come with me, and she still had mixed emotions about the whole thing. But the family was with me.

We were met at the airport by a gray navy van with "US Navy" on the side of it in large block letters. A chief petty officer was the driver, and beside him sat a young ensign, in charge. The ensign greeted me and the family. He was a young lad from Texas who had been over here for a year and still talked with a slow Texas drawl. Colleen thought he was cute.

After loading the luggage, the family piled into the van and headed north from Shannon for the base, which was a few hundred miles away, almost at the tip of Northern Ireland. It was a mild summer afternoon in late July with patches of thick clouds scattered across the blue sky. All the passengers had their faces pressed against the windows of the van. The green quilt work of the Irish countryside moved past the windows. Dairy cows grazed on the thick green grass. Small farms dotted the countryside. Every so often, the van had to stop for a farmer leading his sheep or cattle across the road. The children loved this. It was almost like being inside a postcard for Ireland. We passed through a number of small villages with houses painted in bright hues. Every now and then there was a thatched roof home or a tall stone fortress or castle off in the distance.

"This looks like the land where hobbits live," said Tara.

"I never knew there were so many shades of green," said Mary. "My dad was so right."

We continued north toward Derry as the sun dropped lower in the sky, the countryside changing from farms to more industry. The towns took on a grayer color. The bright-colored buildings from the first part of our trip were not so inviting anymore. Even the weather began to change as the puffy white clouds turned dark gray and covered the sun.

When twilight was beginning to fall, the van slowed down and came to a stop.

"Border into Northern Ireland," said the chief petty officer. "British troops. This'll only take a minute, Captain."

A few young, dour-looking British troops in green uniforms with weapons drawn peered into the van and politely asked for passports from everyone. Tara clutched her hobbit, and Colleen glared back. I gave the driver all of our passports. The British soldiers looked at me and saluted. Then the British troops raised the gate across the road and waved the van on.

The sudden stop and inspection put a damper on the lighthearted journey north from Shannon.

"What was that all about?" Mary asked.

"They're checking for guns coming into Northern Ireland," said the chief petty officer. "But they shouldn't bother us anymore."

"Guns" Shawn questioned.

"Guns for the IRA," said the driver, "in their battle with the Unionists."

Mary looked at me.

"You never told me about a war going on," she said.

I waved my hand in a dismissive manner.

"Not a war," I said, "just a minor skirmish."

I whispered into Mary's ear so that the driver could not hear and refute my claim. But I wondered how much longer I could keep the real danger of the situation from her.

Ever since I was given this assignment, I had to painfully manage a constant inner pressure and keep all the danger to myself. Every time I looked at Mary's and the children's faces, I had to take a deep breath and fight my emotions. It was gut wrenching not to talk with Mary about my feelings. I wondered over and over if it was a smart idea to take the family with me into such a dangerous situation. Maybe I should have left them at home in Virginia.

But I hated being away from them and felt that if I had come to Northern Ireland alone, it might be the end of my marriage. I resolved not to think about the dangers and keep those fears in check. But keeping these feelings to myself created a relentless mental pressure cooker.

Crossing the border into Northern Ireland was like crossing into another world. The town of Strabane was right inside the border of Northern Ireland, and it looked like a bombed-out city from World War II. British troops wearing berets patrolled the streets, and tanks could be seen in a number of places. Many windows in the shops were broken, and barbed wire blocked some of the streets.

"What happened here?" asked Mary.

"Strabane suffered extensive damage from the beginning of the troubles in the early 1970s," the driver said. "The Nationalists and the IRA regularly attacked the town's constabulary and the British Army."

The children were frightened. Tara pushed up against me and Colleen against her mother. Shawn was appalled by the destruction. "Dad, how could people destroy the factories they need for their jobs?" asked Shawn.

Mary glanced at me to see how I was going to answer Shawn, but I just shrugged. I didn't have an answer.

Outside of Letterkenny and west of Strabane there was countryside dotted with the lights of farmhouses as the twilight moved into evening. Soon, the road ran along a river.

"The River Foyle," said the driver. "Almost at the base, Captain."

However, the van was stopped again by more soldiers at the checkpoint leading to the Derry Bridge, which crossed the River Foyle. The driver showed the soldiers our ID and passports, and the soldiers snapped to a salute.

The van soon left the river and continued up a long, winding hill. It then leveled out on a large plateau. Down below, the lights of Londonderry were twinkling in the dark of the night, and we heard the sounds of distant sirens from the city across the river.

The road followed a long fence, which bordered the naval base. Along the fence were signs that read, "US Navy Property." Soon, the van came to a stop at a gate with a guardhouse, and an elderly gentleman, dressed in a dark uniform and cap, came out, looked in the van, and then saluted.

"Welcome to NAVCOMMSTA Londonderry, Captain," the guard said.

I saluted back from inside the van.

"Thank you, sir," he said.

The van continued through the gate and took a sharp right. We could see many homes and buildings that were no more than black shapes in the night. Not far from the gate, the van pulled up in front of a beautiful brick ranch home with a small yard in the front.

"Your new home, Captain," the ensign announced.

They carried our luggage into the house, and the children were quick to claim their bedrooms. The home was smaller than our new home in Springfield, Virginia, and the appliances were older and the furniture worn. I noticed that Mary was not saying much as she surveyed our new quarters.

"We'll fix it up," I said, squeezing her shoulders. "Some fresh paint and new carpet, you'll see."

But she was not so easily convinced.

There was a phone call, and I answered it.

"This is Captain Barker," the voice said. "Welcome to the base, Tom. After your long trip, I know the family must be very tired. We put some food in the refrigerator for you. Why don't we meet in your new office tomorrow at ten? I'm sending Chief Warrant Officer James Emberton to pick you up. He'll be at your place a little before ten. I'll show you around the office. We've planned a welcome barbecue for you and your family tomorrow evening at your place. We'll do all the cooking and everything. There'll be a number of your senior officers there with their wives and children."

"Thank you, Captain Barker," I said. "I look forward to meeting you tomorrow."

Chapter 5

The Office

A little before ten o'clock the next morning, there was a knock on the door. I opened it to see a freckle-faced warrant officer with red hair and a playful smile on his face.

"Warrant Officer James Emberton," he said, straightening up and giving a salute.

I saluted back.

"How long have you been stationed here, Jim?" I asked on our short drive to the office.

"Nearly two years, sir; my orders were for a year, but I asked for an extension. My wife's from Scotland, and we like to visit her family once in a while."

"Like it over here?" I asked.

"Hard not to like it, Captain; the Irish love us Yanks, and the feeling is mutual."

"Where ya from, Jimmy?"

"A little town in Tennessee, sir."

"Over here must be a little different from your home."

"It's as different as it can get, but I love it, especially the many golf courses."

"Even with the troubles going on?"

"No one likes the troubles, Captain. It just seems to be one of those facts of life in these parts. We all gotta get used to it."

Jimmy Emberton pulled into the office parking lot, and I followed him into the office. Inside, the office was buzzing with the sound of teletypes clicking and telephones ringing. As I entered, everyone immediately stood up and saluted; I saluted back.

Captain Paul Barker, the current commanding officer (CO), came over to me. He was a small, wiry man with a crew cut, who, I heard was not much of a people person.

"Welcome aboard, Captain," Captain Barker said.

He then introduced me to Moira McGuffy, his new secretary. Moira was an attractive redheaded woman with blue eyes. She was somewhere in her late thirties.

"Moira was born and raised in Londonderry," Captain Barker explained. "Been on the base for ten years; your success here depends on Moira's confidence and support."

There was laughter in the room.

"I hope that won't be too hard to earn," I said and smiled at Moira.

"And next to Moira is Shannon Kelly," said Captain Barker. "Shannon is Moira's assistant and handles things when Moira gets bogged down. She's studying to be an accountant."

Shannon was somewhere in her late twenties. She had an infectious smile, pale white skin, and the traditional dark-brown hair.

Captain Barker then introduced me to Lieutenant Commander Bob McManus. "Bob is your executive officer."

"Good to have you here, Captain," McManus said, saluting. "We've been looking forward to having you here."

Captain Barker introduced me to a few other civilian employees in the office who had various administrative tasks.

Then we went into my new office and closed the door. It was a corner office with large windows on both sides. One window faced east, and a streak of morning sunshine came through it and fell on the center of a good-sized mahogany office desk. We walked around the office, examining the contents of the file drawers and the intercom system. He then pointed to a stack of boxes in the corner of the office.

"Your files arrived yesterday," he said. Then he handed me a small key.

"This is the key to your classified filing cabinet. Good idea to always keep it locked these days with all the classified communications we're getting from the Pentagon. Didn't used to be like this, but the "troubles" have changed a lot of things, as I'm sure you're already aware."

He sat down behind the desk and motioned for me to sit down. He placed his hands on the desk and surveyed the room.

"I know you've been briefed by the admiral on the situation here," he said.

"Yes," I said.

"Things keep intensifying," Captain Barker said. "It's impossible for outsiders to know how much hatred is just outside the gates of this base."

Chapter 6

Captain Barker's Scoop

Barker pulled out a notebook and opened it. "We keep a record of the violence here in Northern Ireland," he said as he began to read from the notebook. "July has seen an increasing amount of violence. On July 2, six civilians (five Protestants and one Catholic) were killed near Antrim. On July 8, the Ulster Freedom Fighters killed a Catholic civilian. On July 9, two Catholic citizens (a husband and wife) were killed by the Ulster Freedom Fighters. On July 17, two IRA members were killed in Castledown. On July 21, a British soldier was killed from a booby-trapped bomb on a nearby British Army base in Derry. On July 26, Christopher Ewart Biggs, the British ambassador to Ireland, was killed in a landmine attack on his official car in Sandyford, Dublin. His secretary, Judith Cook, was also killed in the explosion. On July 29, three Catholic civilians were killed as a result of a bomb attack on Whitefort Inn, Andersonstown Road, Belfast. And on July 30, four Protestant civilians died as a result of a gun attack on the Stag Inn, Belfast."

Captain Barker closed the notebook.

"And so it goes," he said. "But I'm sure there's much more I don't know about."

"Hard to believe the hatred between Catholics and Protestants," I said. "So different from the States."

Captain Barker dismissed this by waving his hand. "The Catholics and Protestants in the States haven't been around for a thousand years like they have in Ireland," he said.

Captain Barker then placed his hand on a white telephone on the side of the desk.

"Just added this," he said. "A phone directly to Admiral Perry's office at the headquarters of Commander in Chief Naval Forces, Europe (CINCNAVEUR). The admiral insisted on the phone until the base is closed down. He wants you to let him know immediately about any incidents affecting the base or personnel. Also, Admiral Schmidt wants an update call every week. This whole place is a hot political football with the presidential election coming up and the State Department trying to figure out what the hell our stance toward Northern Ireland should be. President Ford swept the whole thing under the rug more or less, but that great humanitarian president, Carter, wants us out of Northern Ireland. It's a delicate situation to say the least. The sooner the base can be handed back to the British, the better."

"I've been in delicate situations before," I replied.

"I know; I've seen your career records," said Captain Barker. "But I don't think you've been in any situation as delicate as this."

"It seems like a rather straightforward assignment: close down the communications station, turn the property back over to the British, while at the same time, expand the communication facilities in Thurso, Scotland, all without incident."

Captain Barker shook his head in disagreement.

"Don't get lulled into how peaceful everything seems to be on the base. The base is entangled with the city of Londonderry in ways you'll see. Over its thirty-five years here, a third of the sailors have married local girls, and there is almost an equal number of Catholic and Protestant civilians on the base. Nothing behind the fences on the base is separated very much from the "troubles" in Londonderry and throughout Northern Ireland. Things are not always as they appear."

"I appreciate the information, Captain," I said. "But still, I'm here to simply close a base down and turn it back to Her Majesty, the Queen."

"Those are major challenges you have," Captain Barker said. "They're not insignificant ones. The fact is that hardly anyone wants to see the base closed down. It means too much to jobs in the area. It's become the livelihood for hundreds of families, both Catholic and Protestant. But even more than this, the Catholics, and particularly the militant branch of Catholics, the IRA, do not want to see it closed down and then possibly turned over to you know who—the plan Admiral Schmidt briefed you on at the meeting in his office."

Captain Barker stood up and began walking toward the office door.

"This base is still an important communications line for submarines with its VLF transmissions. However, with the new satellite communication technology, things can soon be done with half the personnel and cost of the past."

Before his departure, Captain Barker gestured toward the stack of boxes in the corner of the office.

"You have a lot of things to go through," he said. "Talk to Moira if you need anything or have any questions. We've got a nice little welcome party planned for you and the family tonight. Give you a chance to meet your senior officers and personnel. The mess crew is setting everything up and bringing everything. No need to do any work. Just get acquainted with the office. I'll see you at the party."

When Captain Barker was gone, I went over and took the seat behind his desk. I just sat there awhile, thinking about the things Barker had told me. I was surprised that Barker spoke so matter-of-factly about turning the base over to the British Army when so many people depended on it for their livelihood. Scuttlebutt had it that Captain Barker was heading for a position shuffling papers at the Pentagon like I had been doing. Barker seemed to want the paper-pushing job as much as I wanted out of it.

I got up, went over, and looked out the window that faced north toward other buildings on the base. Like the main office, it had the look of other bases I had seen before. There was a large brown-brick building that I was sure was the gymnasium, where much of the social life of the base would be, and a small, squat building I was sure was the officer's club. There were the long buildings I recognized as barracks for the enlisted men and women. There were also very nice houses on the base for the senior officers and married sailors with families.

Here and there, a jeep went past, and somewhere nearby, I could hear the sound of a baseball game in progress. Some navy wives chatted over a few baby strollers.

I began opening the boxes, putting the files away, and organizing my desk. It was hard to believe the immediate and horrifying danger that lurked in and around this base.

That afternoon, after reading through a number of memos and filing papers away, I decided to walk home from the office. It was late afternoon, and the sun had dropped behind some of the buildings on the western part of the base, making long shadows fall from the tall antenna structures. Off in the distance, I could hear sirens and machine-gun fire. Memories of Vietnam.

Chapter 7

Welcome Party

There was a flurry of activity at home. A number of women were unrolling a long red-white-and-blue banner over the door that said, "Welcome McKeown Family!" in big navy-blue letters. The children were playing with some other kids in the street. Shawn was tossing a baseball back and forth with a few other guys. Inside, some personnel from the mess hall were busy putting out snacks on tables, supervised by Mary. She looked much happier and less tentative than she had last night, and I could see that she had a happy expression on her face. I kissed her and continued to survey the hectic scene. Outside, a few large grills were being set up, and next to them, a hefty man was setting up a bar.

"Carl Campbell, Captain," the big man said, extending a plump hand. "I'm the bartender at the officer's club."

"Nice to meet you, Carl. Sounds like you might be right in the center of a lot of the scuttlebutt on base."

The big man laughed.

"Twenty years of scuttlebutt," said Carl. "Came here in the mid 1950s right out of grade school."

"I might have to call on you over the next few months," I said and smiled. "Keep me updated on what's really going on at the base."

"Absolutely, Captain, anytime," Carl said.

"I imagine there is a lot of scuttlebutt flying around these days with Captain Barker leaving and me coming aboard," I said.

"You know sailors," said Carl. "They like to speculate on things. That's the way they are. You know all about that, Captain."

"What's the big topic of speculation?" I asked.

The large bartender glanced around the yard. Apart from a few guys setting up the grills, we were alone.

"Oh you know," said Carl. "About all types of things that are usually just talk."

"Like what?" I asked.

"Like the fact that Captain Barker is a Protestant and you're a Catholic, by God, an Irish Catholic to boot!"

"Why is this so important? It means little where I come from."

The big man poured a pint of Guinness and pushed it across the bar toward me.

"It means everything over here, Captain, and we share the same religion," he said. "Especially with the troubles, ya know. Talk is that the navy brass feel more secure with an Irish Catholic like yourself running the base than a Protestant."

"That's ridiculous."

"Aye! It might sound ridiculous right now, but wait till you've been here for a while. As I said, I hear all types of foolish talk in my job. Sometimes it's just too many pints of Guinness talkin', Captain."

Just then, Captain Barker came into the backyard followed by a number of other people. The grills were operating, and hamburgers were sizzling; the familiar smell made me think for a moment that I was home back in the States. Children were scurrying about the backyard and already forming a line for the hamburgers. The sun had disappeared, and the lights from colorful lanterns that rimmed the perimeter of the backyard gave a festive ambiance to the evening. I could see Mary come from the middle of a huddle of other wives. She was laughing and enjoying her new friends. Someone had even brought a record player, and that pervasive song "In the Still of the Night" was played. It seemed impossible to escape the song and the disco music of the times.

"I see you've met Carl," said Captain Barker. "You have to watch out for Carl. He has the goods on everyone."

A ripple of laughter went through the group around Captain Barker.

"You've already met your XO, Bob McManus," said Barker, pushing the young lieutenant commander forward out of the group. "Bob knows how to get things done around here—been indispensable to me."

"I'm sure he'll be a lot of help to me," I said.

"George O'Donnell here is the senior civilian employee on the base. George has been on the base longer than anyone. He was here when it started in 1941. Some say he was born on the base. Knows more about things than anyone."

There was a short ripple of laughter.

"He even met the queen," said Captain Barker.

"Aye! You're forgetting Bob Hope and Joey Heatherton!" said George.

"Of course," said Captain Barker.

"It's a pleasure to meet ye, Captain," George said, extending his hand to me. "Just let me know anything you need, any questions you might have. If I can't answer them, I'll get someone who can."

"Thanks, George. I'll have a lot of questions, I'm sure."

"You've already met Warrant Officer Jimmy Emberton," said Barker. "Jimmy's an expert in the supply business, is the official tour guide, and is a hell of a golfer."

I smiled.

"And last but certainly not least is Ian Nelson. He heads up the finances of the base. Knows where all the money comes from and goes. Been on the base for ten years. Anything involving money goes through Mr. Nelson."

I looked at Ian. He was a tall, slender man somewhere in his sixties with white hair and a large white handlebar mustache. He was meticulously dressed in a black suit with a white starched shirt and a garish-looking tangerine-colored patterned tie. It was blinding. Among the officers dressed that night in colorful, casual clothing, he stood out like a black spider on a piece of angel food cake.

The unique-looking man extended his hand.

"Welcome, Captain," he said. "You've got a challenge ahead of you."

"Next, is Lieutenant Tom Johnson," said Captain Barker. "Tom is our operations officer. He is in charge of all the communications, radios, antennas, relay center, and receiver and transmission sites."

"How ya doin, Captain? I hear ya from New Joisey. I'm from da Bronx. Who knew?" said Lieutenant Johnson.

"Nice to meet you," I said. "I'll be depending on you."

"Finally, I would like to introduce you to Senior Chief Charlie Wilson. He is our chief master-at-arms. He wholeheartedly represents the black community on the base, and we are extremely proud of him. Well, that does it for your key people. Everyone enjoy the evening," said Barker.

Music from the record player flowed over the backyard and the colored lights, playing songs popular in the States at the time: Paul Simon's "Fifty Ways to Leave Your Lover"; "Silly Love Songs," by Paul McCartney and Wings; and "Sara Smile," by Hall and Oates.

I walked around introducing myself to the people at the party. My secretary, Moira, was there with her husband. Shannon Kelly was there by herself, explaining to me that her husband, Sean, was home watching the kids.

"Should have brought them along," I said to Shannon.

She looked at me, and the hint of a smile came to her face but was quickly gone.

"Maybe," she said. "It's not that easy."

The kids were attacking the hamburgers and hot dogs, and Carl was a busy man pouring pints of Guinness at the bar. After a while, speech became a little slurred, and talk became looser. Captain Barker was one of the last to say good night.

"You and I have a lot of things to finish up over here before I head back to the States," he said. "Not the least is our change-of-command ceremony."

"We sure do," I said. "Good night, Paul. See you tomorrow. Thanks for putting together this great welcome party."

I stood by myself, surveying the yard; the red, white, and blue streamers on the grass; and the dangling lanterns now swaying with the hint of an evening breeze.

Out of a dark corner of the yard, a tall, dark shape approached, and the shape turned into the well-dressed Ian Nelson, the gentleman with the blinding orange tie.

"You have a tough, important job ahead of you, Captain," Nelson said in a deliberate accent that was more British than Irish. "Closing this base will not be an easy task."

I was surprised and a little annoyed by these words at such a festive welcoming event.

"Doing anything important is never easy," I said to Nelson.

"Important the base ends up in the right hands," Nelson replied.

"The queen will take good care of it, I'm sure," I said.

"What does the queen know about Northern Ireland?" Ian replied. "She deploys a bunch of troops over here and thinks that will do. Well, it isn't working."

"You have a better idea?" I asked.

"Not me," Ian said. "Others have a better idea."

"And what's the better idea?" I asked.

"It doesn't involve turning the base over to the queen," Ian replied.

As he said this, he disappeared back into the darkness of the night, and I was left to ponder his mysterious comments. I wondered if Ian somehow had information about the turnover of the base to the British Army. He could be a dangerous person if he did. Just then, George O'Donnell, the senior civilian, walked over from the opposite side of the yard to say good night.

I said to George, "That Ian Nelson is a strange bird. Seems like he has a large chip on his shoulder."

"Aye," George said. "A strange one he is. Like a lot of fervent Protestants."

"I don't think he likes me very much," I said.

"He knows yer an Irish Catholic," George said. "That's enough for him. You're the first Irish Catholic to command the base in many years. He's more than a little suspicious about ye."

"And the dark suit and the bright-orange tie? What was that all about?" I asked.

"An Orangeman," said George. "He's been a member of the organization for as long as I've known him."

"What the hell is an Orangeman?" I asked.

"It's a long story, Captain, and I'll tell you sometime," George said. "Basically, they're the radical Protestant version of the Catholic IRA. A nasty group of lads for sure. You always hear the violence up here is between the IRA and the British Army. Truth be told, much of the violence is between IRA and Orangemen."

I walked over to get a final pint from Carl, who was closing up the bar.

"Let me buy you one more," I said to George.

"Of course, Captain. I'm dying of the thirst watching all the others pour it down."

"Here's to a new friend," I said, raising my pint toward George.

"And here's to a fellow Irish Catholic taking command of the base," George said with a twinkle in his eye.

When the lights were taken down and everyone was gone and the place cleaned up, Mary and I sat out in the yard in some aluminum chairs. Mary excitedly talked about all the new friends she had made. The wives had all types of clubs and were constantly busy with projects. And the kids had made some nice friends to play with.

Overhead in the sky was one of the most magnificent sights we had ever seen. The greenish-yellow northern lights made the heavens seem like the inside of some great disco club. We had heard about the northern lights but had never witnessed them like tonight.

Mary took my hand.

"I think all that is a sign of something new for us," she said. "A new life. A new family. A new marriage."

I ran my hand through Mary's golden-blond hair.

"I think so too," I said.

I got up from my chair and walked to the edge of the new yard. I looked out over my command like the captain of a ship looking out over the ocean. The buildings on the base were no more than dark shapes briefly illuminated by the rhythmic pulsations of the northern lights.

"I feel like I've got command of a ship again," I said to Mary.

"Does it feel good?" she snidely asked.

I walked back to her, leaned over, and kissed her.

My heart was pounding. I felt terribly guilty to have to close this base, and to put Mary and my little ones in danger. On top of all this, I had to keep secret the transfer of the base to the British Army. All of these things were tearing my insides apart.

Chapter 8

Change of Command

As was customary, I had a meeting with my commissioned officers and senior enlisted chief petty officers—altogether, a total of twenty-seven—who were in charge of various departments and operations of the base. I was able to set forth my personal policies on leadership and explain upcoming changes for our operations. All of the officers were aware of the pending closure of the base.

The change-of-command ceremony is a tradition in the US Navy. It is attended by all hands, spouses, dignitaries, and invited guests, such as the mayor, council members, and media.

Full dress uniforms is the protocol for officers and crew, including large, shiny medals and pristine white gloves. The tradition of the wearing of swords dates back to the era of white-winged clipper ships when combat was hand to hand as ships came alongside each other in battle. A navy honor guard would also be present in full regalia and well rehearsed for their role in the ceremony.

Captain Barker and I proudly wore our medals. The one most meaningful to me was the Combat Meritorious medal I received after my tour in Vietnam for extraordinary leadership and bravery.

Starting from left to right, Captain McKeown at the podium,
Reverend Nash, Lieutenant Commander Bob McManus,
the mayor of Londonderry, and Father Mullins.

The base gym was decorated to the max with red, white, and blue streamers, almost giving the big brown-brick building an element of personality. According to tradition, on stage was seated Admiral Schmidt, the big boss, who had selected me for the dubious assignment. Next to him sat Captain Barker and then me. The meager navy band was playing marching music in the background. A local Protestant minister acted as chaplain, and Lt. Commander Bob McManus served as master of ceremonies. The color guard presented the colors. All in attendance stood and placed their hands over their hearts as the band played "The Stars and Stripes." The color guard then retired the colors.

The chaplain began, "All who are gathered here are joined in one desire: to wish the newly arriving Captain McKeown the blessings of our Heavenly Father for his prudent leadership in his new assignment."

I thought to myself, *I'm going to need all the help I can get.*

At this point, Admiral Schmidt was introduced. The admiral called Captain Barker and me to the podium and handed us a copy of our orders, which, in turn, we read aloud. The admiral stood quite erect between us, like a statue in the park.

After reading my orders, I turned smartly on my heel, saluted Captain Barker, and announced in a loud voice, "I hereby relieve you, sir."

He returned my salute and responded with equal volume, "I stand relieved, sir."

The official part of the ceremony now concluded, my emotions and thoughts tumbled over each other. *That's it...I'm in the driver's seat now. What a hell of a job this is going to be!* Then I noticed the admiral's grin as he grabbed the microphone. "Congratulations are in order to Captain Barker on his accomplishments at this naval base. I personally wish him and his family all the best in his next assignment."

Captain Barker stood still while a navy commendation medal was pinned to his uniform. The admiral and Captain Barker exchanged salutes.

Admiral Schmidt addressed the audience. "Your newly named base commander, Captain Thomas McKeown, has a most difficult job ahead of him. The US Navy is confident he is well qualified to handle the stressful challenges before him. I know all of you officers and sailors will assist him to the maximum. I caution all of you to be alert and careful, as this is admittedly a dangerous and politically charged environment." He closed, "The entire US Navy is behind all of you and ready to assist in this dangerous and sad endeavor of closing such a wonderful base."

A loud round of applause followed the admiral's address. The participants began their descent from the stage and proceeded to the grassy area below for the reception. I came down from the stage and took Mary's hand, and we proceeded toward the crowd. Mary looked so beautiful in her green and gold formal gown. I surely hoped she would be happy here and find new friends among the other wives.

At the reception, Admiral Schmidt approached us. Mary courteously excused herself and joined the group of wives at the refreshment table.

"Things are really beginning to stir up in Washington," the admiral said.

"In what way?" I asked.

Schmidt replied, "The president and the secretary of state are on my back. They want all Americans out of Northern Ireland ASAP.

The secretary of state has notified the American consulate in Belfast and the contract employees from General Electric to start packing. The point is, Tom, Great Britain is our closest ally, and the president does not want an American to get injured or killed."

I replied, "Based on my initial review of things, I don't see too much of a problem of shutting down the base in nine to twelve months and having Thurso up and running."

I looked briefly around to make sure we were alone.

"However," I said, "there will be great resentment and anger, even violence, if they find out the base is being turned over to the British Army."

"You're right about the potential for violence if this leaks out," said the admiral. "It has to be kept secret at all costs."

The officer's club on the base was packed half an hour after the formal ceremony at the base gymnasium. Carl Campbell was busy pouring drinks and making up his famous Irish concoctions. There was a bar legend that leprechauns drank his brews, which had been perfected over a twenty-year career as chief bartender at the navy base.

It wasn't a minor achievement for sure that Carl was held in high regard around the base as a man you could trust with secrets. How many could you even imagine being able to trust these days?

Carl filled the third pint of beer for me, and I proposed a toast to Captain Barker, who joined us. And there was that song by the Righteous Brothers that followed me everywhere, playing over the jukebox.

Captain Barker stood up and proposed a toast to the new Commanding Officer "and the great challenge he is about to take on."

After his toast, Captain Barker pulled me over into a private corner of the club, away from all the celebrations.

"Tom, there are some notches in your career to be gained for you in Londonderry. It's not going to be a place just to tread water until Scotland. The base is a political hot potato and a lurking time bomb. Your biggest challenge will be getting our people out of Derry without getting anyone killed."

"And closing down a longtime institution in the city that's part of the lives of so many and putting a lot of people out of work. It's amazing the love affair between the city and the base I've seen in the short time I've been here. So many marriages and families resulting from the base. It's become another Derry suburb almost. I've seen this everywhere this past week. The navy has made a major contribution to the economy of the city. The troubles threaten everything now and have been a drain on the city. When the Americans leave, things will become even worse."

Barker got up to leave.

"I'm gonna get some of my files back at the old office. I'm leaving tomorrow for DC."

Captain Barker looked at me. "Let me be straight with you," he said, pointing a heavy finger toward me. It was not too hard to figure out Captain Barker should not have more than a few pints of beer at one time. But what the heck. It was time for celebration, as he was finally getting out of this hellish situation.

"From the outside, this looks like a job to just tread water until the turnover. But looks can be deceiving. Just watch yourself."

When Captain Barker was gone, George and Jimmy wandered over and congratulated me.

"Even though I'm Irish Catholic," I said to George and Jimmy, "it's hard as hell for me to understand the hatred between the Catholics and Protestants."

"I wouldn't expect you to unless you've lived here all your life," George said. "But it's not all that complicated. Northern Ireland has drifted a long way from what it truly is. And, as Orwell once said, the further a society drifts from the truth, the more it hates those who speak it."

I pondered what George just said for a few seconds and then excused myself. I wanted to say a final good-bye to Captain Barker before he left.

⌒⁊⋀⋋

I shook a few more hands and left the officer's club. I escorted Mary home to stay with the children and walked back to my office. Back at the office building, Barker was putting papers into filling boxes. It was an unusually warm summer evening, and the office window was open.

We were not aware that, outside the office, Shannon Kelly was making her way to her car to drive home, when she heard a conversation coming from the office and moved to a position under the window to listen.

Barker said, "I got a threatening call the other day from the IRA." He shook his head with a slight smile. "I got a few when the base closing was first announced a few months ago," he added. "There's a lot of bad feeling. But there is nothing to worry about as long as they don't know what our real plan is."

"I'll keep it from them," I said.

"It'll get harder and harder to do," Barker warned. "There is a growing suspicion all over the place. It is a delicate situation. We outwardly proclaim we're turning the base back to the queen when we really plan on turning it over to the British Army. The Catholics are not in love with the queen, but they have a certain forced acceptance of her. They have none for the British Army. They must never know it is going to the British Army."

These words were all that Shannon Kelly needed to hear. She quickly ran toward the end of the building so as not to be seen and raced to her car.

Chapter 9

The Tour

A week after the welcome party, my daily routine began to materialize. There was the daily briefing from McManus, the XO, and there were phone calls to make and letters to dictate. There was much to learn, and the days were busy, but I enjoyed this type of hands-on work more than pushing papers at the Pentagon.

My green Chevy Vega had not yet arrived from the States so Jimmy Emberton became a temporary chauffeur for the family, taking Mary shopping for things in downtown Londonderry and chaperoning the children around the base. The kids loved his southern Tennessee drawl. Shawn had already found a baseball team on the base, and Colleen was busy with one of her science projects. Tara asked Jimmy if he had ever seen a real hobbit. Jimmy told her he had and they were all over the place.

One overcast afternoon, the slow-talking Tennessean appeared in the parking lot, driving the official base jeep and wearing his usual grin.

We drove past the two-story brick buildings that were the quarters for married servicemen. We stopped at the large Samson Hall, which included the gymnasium.

Next to the gym were the athletic fields, and we walked over and watched the base soccer team practicing. They looked like good athletes, but it was obvious they knew little about soccer.

"As I said, our base soccer team sucks," Jimmy said. "Always getting our butts kicked by the teams in town. One of the real embarrassments of the base. The base has traditionally fielded a soccer team that represented the base locally and in surrounding towns, like Strabane, Dungiven, and Buncrana. Our base teams have never been competitive against local competition. It just isn't our game. But they're ready to learn more about soccer if anyone can show them. I can sense that change is in the air."

"Change?" I asked.

"The guys are getting tired of getting their asses kicked all the time," Jimmy said. "Some of the more experienced members of the squad have decided they want to match up against teams from outside the base."

"Anything being done about it?" I asked.

"There's a great soccer coach available," Jimmy said. "Senior Chief Charlie Wilson, our master-of-arms, is a world-class soccer player. He played for several navy bases, including the major navy base at Norfolk, Virginia."

I filed this information away but did not say anything.

We got back in the jeep and drove down the road a few hundred yards. Jimmy waved his arm to the right.

"There's the mess hall and exchange," he said. "I'm in charge of those places. I'm also in charge of the commissary, payroll, and purchasing. Ian Nelson reports to me on base expenses."

"Tell me about Ian Nelson," I said.

Jimmy paused thoughtfully. "Another time, Captain," he said. "I don't want to take anything away from our tour."

We rode down the street until it turned into a dirt road and then into a thirty-acre field with arrays of hundred-foot-tall antennas. Wires were strung from pole to pole in what looked like a gigantic spider web.

"The bread and butter of the base," Jimmy said. "Very low frequency antennas that transmit to and listen to our submerged North Atlantic submarines, twenty-four/seven. They can hear a sub cough hundreds of feet under the surface of the ocean. As you know, the base is also a critical communications relay station for our fleet of ships, transmitting messages for the Baltic Sea and Mediterranean Sea regions and around the world. We use high-frequency antennas for that mission."

We got out of the jeep and walked around the field.

Off to the side of the field was a very long, squat windowless gray building, and we walked toward it.

"Communications center building," Jimmy said as we went in.

It was dim inside, lit with little more than some bare fluorescent light tubes. Tall gray banks of radio units extended in rows like book rows in a library. A number of base personnel sat in front of the big gray radio banks with headphones, listening and entering information and perforated tapes into large computers and teletype machines.

In a few minutes, we were back in the jeep, heading across the field to a hill rising above the base. Jimmy stopped on top of the hill at a pile of tangled metal and scattered bricks and concrete.

"The old base microwave station," he said. "IRA blew it up a few years ago. Someone said to make known their presence."

I stood looking at the pile of rubble for a few moments. It reminded me of Vietnam. I was within another war zone, I thought, but no one called it that.

"Any other attacks on the base since then?"

"No," Jimmy said. "But there have been a number of threats."

We walked back to the jeep and got in.

"That's really about it, Captain," said Jimmy. "There's the transmitters out at Dungiven, but that's a good distance away and something for another day. There is also a receiver site at Roscommon."

We drove back to my office. George O'Donnell was just coming out of his office.

"I see that Jimmy's giving you the standard tour of the base," he said.

"He's a good tour guide," I said.

"If you have a little more time," George said, "I can extend the tour for you."

"Why not?" I said.

With this, George O'Donnell got into the backseat of the jeep.

"Head downtown," George said to Jimmy.

In a few minutes, we passed through the base gate and headed down the hill and then over the Derry Bridge across the River Foyle into downtown Londonderry.

Jimmy pointed out a few practical things, like shopping areas, but mostly, he gave a running commentary on his favorite pubs.

"So how did you ever decide to come to Ireland from Tennessee?" I asked Jimmy.

Jimmy laughed. "My Scottish bride wanted to be close to her family. She is able to visit by just taking the Strabane ferry across the Irish Sea," he said.

In a minute or so, George told Jimmy to stop the jeep, and when we were stopped, he waved his hand across the landscape in front of us.

"Derry is the only remaining walled city in Ireland," he said. "It's one of the oldest continuously inhabited places in Ireland. The earliest historical references date to the sixth century, when a monastery was founded here by St. Columba."

The people of the town were going about their business. Some waved at the jeep. The American navy was a familiar part of the town. But signs of the continuing troubles were everywhere you looked. Side streets were blocked with great masses of barbed wire, like great bushels of metal tumbleweed. Tanks and armored vehicles were stationed at corners, and British soldiers, wearing berets and helmets and holding guns, passed by the people without any sign of emotion.

"You wanna make sure you talk up with your American accent down here in town," George said. "Otherwise, they get real suspicious of you. Everybody's suspicious of everybody these days."

"Head on out to the Bogside area," George told Jimmy.

We drove out of downtown, and before long, we were in a suburb with narrow little streets and rows of slim, similar flats squeezed so close to each other it looked like one of them would pop out.

"The Bogside area," George said. "Poor Irish-Catholic slums. Where Bloody Sunday happened in seventy-two. Really the place where the troubles took a turn for the worse."

George told Jimmy to stop the jeep in front of a long two-story brick building of flats, each with their chimney on the roof. George got out and motioned for us to follow him. We walked past the flats to the end of them, and then Jimmy pointed up to the wall of the end flat. Written in large block letters on it was the phrase "You Are Now Entering Free Derry."

"We're really at the center of where the troubles started," George said.

I did not say anything but simply looked up at the bold writing on the wall. Only an Irishman, a Catholic Northern Irishman for that matter, could have any real understanding of what they actually meant. It made you feel as if you were Irish Catholic from Northern Ireland. I wasn't from Northern Ireland, but then all my ancestors were from Ireland. So coming to Ireland had had some strange effect on me that I could feel hovering over these first few days at this new base with my family with me. It was a funny, ubiquitous feeling that I could not quite define. In a strange way, I felt that I had arrived at my ancestral home after all of my worldly travels.

As I stood there, looking up at the wall on that summer day, my first week in Londonderry, there was a type of growing realization of this symbolic coming home, so to speak. What was it though? I knew it was there. It seemed thick as an Irish bog at times, as heavy as the Irish mist in Londonderry. Could it be because I was an Irish Catholic? But always, it was some general presence simply hovering around me, like that emotional and expressive song "The Town I Loved So Well" by Phil Coulter seemed to do. You knew something was there. But this was about all the evidence I was given. It was something that fought definition. Perhaps it was my Irish blood rumbling inside of me.

As we stood there under the "Free Derry" sign that day, there was the ringing of bells in the distance—perhaps from the old monastery in town. And somewhere, fading slowly in and out, we could hear a band, just a fiddle and a bagpipe and a few other instruments, playing the song from the city "Derry Air," commonly known as "Danny Boy."

As the song faded away, George began, "A tragic incident, sometimes called the Bogside Massacre, occurred on January 30, 1972, just four years ago, in this very place. An incident right here where we are in the Bogside area of Derry. On this day, twenty-six unarmed civil rights soldiers of the British Army shot protesters and bystanders. Thirteen males, seven of whom were teenagers, died immediately or soon after, while the death of another man four and a half months later was attributed to the injuries he received on that day. Two protesters were also injured when army vehicles ran them down. Five of those wounded were shot in the back. The incident occurred during a

Northern Ireland Civil Rights Association march; the soldiers involved were members of the First Battalion of the Parachute Regiment."

"Have there been any investigations about the event?" I asked.

George O'Donnell laughed at this question. "Of course, there have been investigations," he said. "But it is always a matter of who is doing the investigating. Like everything else in life. The Widgery Tribunal, held in the immediate aftermath of the event, largely cleared the soldiers and British authorities of blame. Widgery described the soldiers shooting as 'bordering on reckless,' but the whole thing was widely criticized as a whitewash."

"What do you think happened that day?" I asked George.

"I don't think what happened," George said. "I *know* what happened. I was there. There needs to be criminal charges filed against the soldiers involved in the incident. All those shot were unarmed. The killings were unjustified. Innocent people were murdered, innocent Irish Catholics. There needs to be criminal charges against the British soldiers, and the British prime minister needs to make an apology on behalf of the United Kingdom."

What terrible bitterness over religion, I thought. How crazy is that? They both worship God. I wondered what God thought about this. Such a beautiful city. Maybe someday, they'll come to their senses.

We drove back to base. In the late afternoon, most base personnel were at home for dinner. But there he was. Ian Nelson was watching us go by in the jeep. He was wearing another orange tie and as always dressed like a doorman at some fancy club.

Jimmy stopped in front of the base office building, and George and I got out of the jeep. George said good-bye, as he was late for dinner and the wonderful little "battleax," as he lovingly called his wife, did not like him being late for dinner.

"Thanks for the tour," I said.

"Anytime, Captain," said Jimmy.

As I walked around the side of the jeep, I noticed a golf bag tucked away under the backseat.

"You play golf?" I asked Jimmy.

"Mount Juliet grade school champion in Tennessee," Jimmy said. "Came close to having a college scholarship too but barely missed it because of Vietnam."

I reached out and shook Jimmy's hand.

"Played on every base I've been on," I said. "Even brought a three iron with me to Nam."

"We've gotta play Royal Portrush," Jimmy said. "It's only ten miles north from here on the coast, one of the greatest golf courses in all of Europe."

"Yes, of course," I said. "I've heard of it. Go ahead and plan something on a weekend a few weeks off."

"Aye, aye, sir," Jimmy said with that big smile on his face.

Chapter 10

Signs of Intimidation

It was late afternoon, and the office was empty except for Willard McIver, a large Irish guy, who worked as a cleaning person after hours. You could almost smell dank Guinness or Jameson's on his breath. I meant to ask Moira or Shannon about Willard, but I kept forgetting.

I waved to Willard, who seemed to be slow dancing an Irish jig with a large broom or mop off in one corner of the office. The big Irishman lifted his arm and waved as he grunted something to me.

I went into my office and opened the door to a closet, revealing a dark-blue golf bag with the words "US Navy" on it in golden letters. I pulled various clubs out of the bag and briefly examined them like troops getting ready to go into battle for another season. Then I pulled the putter out of the bag and some golf balls from one of the zippered pockets. I tossed a few balls onto the dark-green carpet, which was more like rough than a true green. What would those greens at Portrush be like? Much better than the carpet in my office.

I putted the ball toward a make-believe cup on the carpet from different positions.

All of the sudden, my phone rang. This seemed strange. Mary seldom called if I was late, as she had learned better over the years.

"Captain McKeown," said a voice with a thick Irish accent.

"Yes, this is Captain McKeown," I said.

There was a short pause on the phone.

"We want to welcome ye to Northern Ireland," the voice said.

"We?" I said.

"Just some fellow members of the Catholic religion, you know," the voice said. "Some fellow members who have problems with the bloody damned Protestants."

I considered this statement.

"The IRA? Are you a member?" I ventured to ask.

There was a short burst of laughter.

"Aye, the IRA," the voice said. "Just want a fellow Catholic to know he's being watched by other Catholics. Just so you don't do anything foolish."

I responded, "Foolish?"

A short pause again. "Yes, foolish," the voice said. "Like turning the base over to the British Army. Now that would be a very dangerous and a foolish move, Captain. Do ye understand that?"

I was angered by the intimidation of the caller.

"That's ridiculous," I said. "The base is given back to the queen, not the British Army. When did you ever hear of the navy and the army being so congruent in their military outlook?"

There was a pause again on the phone.

"Good night, Captain, and welcome to Northern Ireland."

After the call, I sat and contemplated the threat. I thought of calling Admiral Schmidt in DC but decided not to. *Yes, welcome to Northern Ireland*, I thought to myself. There was the official welcoming party a few nights ago. But this was the real-world welcome. The *unofficial* welcome so to speak. This other welcome created a fear I would be living with the rest of my time on the base.

At home that night, Mary asked about my day.

"Fine," I said. "A great tour of the base by Warrant Officer Emberton."

I didn't mention the phone call to Mary for fear of giving her more ammunition for future conversations, but I did share the trip downtown to the "Free Derry" wall. It was not much different looking than that scary city we had passed a few weeks ago on our way into Ireland. The rest of Ireland seemed picture-postcard worthy, spreading their arms open to the tourist trade.

Mary and I continued our conversation. I described the various shops and a large department store called Austin's located in the city over the bridge. She seemed pleased to hear of shopping opportunities with the ladies. The balance of the day's tour, I kept to myself. Even though Mary was of Irish descent and looking forward to researching her ancestry, Northern Ireland's troubles was a topic I tried to avoid at all costs.

Northern Ireland was different. There was still a great battle going on up there for freedom. I knew I was placed in the middle of it for some reason. Whoever or whatever came first was no longer of any matter, as the two blended stressfully within me. Perhaps this was really the pervasive battle in my life—that battle between definition and nondefinition.

Chapter 11

The Hatchet Man

The base seemed to be happy that Captain Barker was gone. He always seemed like a fish hopelessly out of water. It was the anniversary of my first month in Ireland, and Mary and I left the kids behind for a weekend by ourselves to explore the surrounding countryside and work on building up the marriage. The first month seemed to be a small triumph for me in winning over Mary to the idea that she might actually like a few things about living in Londonderry for a year, especially the new friends and volunteering for Meals on Wheels.

We drove northwest from Londonderry and crossed the border out of Northern Ireland and into Donegal, where we spent a good part of the day in the little fishing village called Moville on the western ocean side of the Republic of Ireland. We acted like the traditional newlywed couple, visiting shops, having lunch next to the ocean, and buying some crabs from a fisherman. This was such a beautiful part of Ireland. We'll have to bring the kids to the beaches.

Before we drove back, we decided to stop at a nearby pub in the village. I was dressed in civilian clothes—a blue polo shirt and jeans. We looked like American tourists. I ordered two pints of Guinness. The bartender picked up my American accent and looked me up and down.

"Aye, aye, Captain McKeown," he said.

Mary and I were startled to be recognized by a bartender in a village over fifty miles from the base.

"How do you know who I am?" I asked.

" Aye, everybody knows this, Captain," he said. "You're the hatchet man. You've come to close the American naval base in Derry."

This was an astounding realization to me, as I never saw myself in this way. But it was an apt description for my unpopular job in Derry. I was there to close a base that had a substantial connection to the economy, and a connection to the people of a city it had been a neighbor with for many years.

We drove back to Londonderry without saying much.

"You're well known," was the only comment that Mary would make on the event, but it was obvious that it was upsetting to her that her husband had a reputation as the hatchet man."

In Londonderry, I searched for the Bogside area of town. I remembered a few things, like the monastery, the wall, and the long, narrow streets of the suburb. I found the row of flats that had the words "Free

Derry" painted on the end of them. I stopped the car, and we got out and began a short walk around the wall. I explained the place but not in the way that George had told me.

⌒⌒

A little girl about Tara's age pushed the window curtain back, watching girls play games on the street in front of her flat and then moving her gaze left down the street to see a man and a woman looking up at the "Free Derry" sign. *Probably Americans*, she thought to herself.

Megan Kelly pulled her wheelchair away from the window and listened to the voices of her parents in the kitchen. It was the same type of screaming she had heard so many times growing up.

The kitchen was in a dark, dingy little flat in the Bogside. A small slant of late-afternoon sunlight came under the shade of the window, which was pulled down most of the way. A dark, cave-like place. Dreary.

Shannon Kelly stood, doing the dishes in the small sink in her tiny kitchen. Her husband, Sean Kelly, paced back and forth in an angry, anxious manner. A number of empty beer bottles lay around the room.

"Phone calls have little effect," he said. "It's just as we suspected all along. We need to take action. Words are not enough."

He picked up the phone and made a call. There were no names used in the call.

"The base is being turned over to the British Army," he said. "Shannon heard the two captains discussing this. There is no doubt about it. We'll have the British Army all over the place."

There was a pause on the phone.

"Yes," Sean said. "Right, we'll get right on it. It's about time we rock the Yanks' world. I can't believe they would do such a thing. That McKeown guy is an Irishman by heritage. An Irish Catholic! He has no idea what we're going through!"

⌐⍋⊶

Mary and I returned to the car and drove across the bridge over the Loch Foyle back to the base.

Chapter 12

Explosive Warning

With Captain Barker gone, all types of rumors were beginning to circulate around the base. Under Captain Barker's command, everything had seemed to float rather aimlessly, like a marooned ship at sea or like someone dog-paddling in water, just staying afloat but not making any progress toward any particular destination. Nothing seemed to be going anywhere. Now, with me in command, I set a course and headed for our final port. There was gripping anxiety and tension in the air.

The closing of the base was not something discussed every day. But it was a hot topic in the evenings at the officer's club. Carl Cameron got an earful of all the talk. My executive officer, Bob McManus, told me he was hearing more and more scuttlebutt around the base. And George O'Donnell stopped by the office one day just shaking his head.

"Things haven't been this tense on the base since the war," he said. "And things were tense as hell then."

I called a meeting of my senior officers to discuss the situation. I set out my personal policies on leadership and explained upcoming changes in base operations. It had been barely a month since my arrival, and things were moving fast.

"I think you need to call a meeting of all the civilian employees on the base," Bob said. "Things need to be addressed and put out in the open. They realize their jobs will be lost."

I agreed, and a general meeting was scheduled for the gymnasium.

A few days later, I stood behind a podium on the little makeshift stage in the gym and looked out over a crowd of a few hundred people. Some of the civilian employees were related to crewmembers as spouses and other dependents. But most were indigenous Northern Ireland citizens. My top officers sat on the stage behind me. A week ago, the stage had been wrapped in red, white, and blue streamers and there was a spirit of celebration with smiling faces and lively, optimistic speeches about the future. But now the red, white, and blue streamers were gone, and there was a dark, dim atmosphere in the gym.

"Welcome, everyone, to our first town-hall meeting," I said. "Prior to arriving here, I was informed by my superiors that the president of the United States personally ordered this base to be closed for the protection of American personnel and their families."

There was some shuffling around in the crowd in front of me. I could sense the tension. No one had heard before how much priority was given to the base closing.

"I am not happy about this mission," I continued. "The past two weeks, I have begun to understand your concerns and anxiety as to what can be expected in the future. The US Navy will do everything possible to help you civilian employees find new jobs as we begin to close down, and I will do everything I can do to help you make this transition. It's a beautiful place here in Londonderry. Our base has a great history of outstanding support to the fleet. Now, please ask your questions, and I'll respond as best I can."

Ian Nelson stood up. He was again dressed in a black suit and wearing a white shirt and an orange tie.

"Captain, I understand that when the base closes, you are going to turn it over to the British Army," Ian Nelson said. "Is this correct?"

I was shocked speechless that Ian would make such a devastating statement in front of all the civilian personnel, comprising both Protestant Loyalists and members of the IRA.

"I have no idea where you got this information, Mr. Nelson," I answered. "We have no intention of turning the base over to the British Army. The property and certain facilities will be returned to Her Majesty, the Queen. It will be her decision as to the disposition of the base. It may return to the city of Derry, where, of course, the housing, gymnasium, and playing fields would be very useful. And the antenna fields could be valuable for growing crops. But may I emphasize one more time, the US Navy's mission is to close the base and return it to the queen."

Ian Nelson only smiled at hearing this, shaking his head in obvious disagreement as he sat down.

There were a number of employees who stood up and told touching stories; civilian employees who had worked on the base most of their lives. I learned quickly that the base was much more than just another job to many employees. It was really a second home for them. There had been so many marriages of American sailors to local girls from Londonderry. There were mixed Irish-American families now. It was a livelihood for fathers and sons, mothers and daughters. It was so much more than just another navy base.

The stories went on for perhaps ten minutes, and I tried to reassure the base civilians that I would do everything I could to find them new jobs. But I came to realize that it was more than just finding new jobs for many of them. I was putting an end to an old friendship and forcing them to find a new way of life.

Suddenly, as if on cue, Ian Nelson stood up and shouted out, "Captain, you're wrong! The base is going to the British Army!"

Simultaneously, a deafening explosion occurred, *boom*, bringing glass and debris down on all of us. The gym shook, and windows shattered. It felt as if the air was sucked right out of my chest. Fluorescent lights fell from the ceiling and dangled on connections while everyone tried to take cover on the floor.

"Oh my God, what's happening?" someone shouted.

"It's a bomb! A bomb!"

People kept screaming. Some shouted out in terror. Quickly glancing around the building, I thought the structure was still intact without serious damage. It was pandemonium and chaos. It was like being back in Nam. What crazy idiot had set this thing off?

My mind was racing over a number of things. It was not the first time I had been in situations like this, and I had an internal checklist I went through. My overall concern was the safety of my personnel.

I wondered, What the hell has happened to our base security? We're really in a combat zone. Bombs and automatic weapons fire had been going on constantly outside the base since I arrived.

People were running for doors to get out of the gym. There was the sound of sirens outside. Soon, base guards were in the gym, conducting a search for any more bombs. British troops also came as well as Irish Gardaí. I wondered how the hell the troops got on the base. With the crisis of the moment, it was something I would have to worry about later.

Bob McManus came up to me.

"Looks like no one is seriously hurt," he said.

"Thank God," I said. "But I don't think it was the intention to hurt anyone, as the bomb went off adjacent to the gym—not directly inside."

"A warning, do ya think?" McManus said.

"Yes," I replied. "A warning."

"From who?" he asked.

"I've got my ideas," I said.

"IRA?"

"It makes sense," I said. "I'll try to find out. I thought they liked us around here. We need to get help."

McManus and I hurried back to the headquarters building, surrounded by a few armed guards. I was worried about the safety of my family and immediately called Mary.

"Oh my God," she said. "I heard the explosion. Are you OK?"

"Yes, fine," I told her. "The kids OK?"

"Yes, but everyone is worried."

"Stay inside," I told Mary. "I'm sending over a guard."

Moira and Shannon Kelly were already in the office, and the telephone was constantly ringing.

"What kind of security do we have on the base?" I asked McManus.

"Not much, Captain," McManus replied. "Four M1s, three M16s, ten pistols, some forty-fives."

"Ridiculous," I said. "We need more weapons and marines."

"I know," he said. "We've tried to get them, but our requests have always been turned down."

"I need to talk to CINCNAVEUR and Admiral Schmidt about this," I said.

I went into my office and closed the door. I tried to put the pieces together. There was the threatening call I received a few days before, and I was pretty sure that the caller's henchmen had made good on this threat. There were the cryptic comments from Ian Nelson at the welcoming party a month before. What did Nelson mean that "others" knew the plans for the base? I suspected it was not a coincidence that the bomb went off immediately following Ian's outburst in the gym.

I picked up the special phone on my desk that had a direct link to Admiral Schmidt's office at the Pentagon.

"Admiral, we've just had an explosion on the base outside the gymnasium. All indications are that it was a bomb blast. Thank God, no one was seriously injured. I'm preparing my official report as we speak. I don't know all the details yet, but I need marines up here as soon as possible to evaluate the security status of this base and also provide necessary support personnel."

"We've already heard about it," said Admiral Schmidt. "Tom, this isn't the first incident we've had at Londonderry. The Provisional IRA blew up the microwave tower close to the armory a few years ago. But the guy ran off the base without any incident. Now, Tom, this is the main issue here. We don't want this bombing to be labeled an 'incident.' The president doesn't want an incident. No one wants an incident."

"What do you mean, sir?" I said in disbelief. "Of course it was an incident."

"No, Captain," the admiral corrected. "It was an event, a minor event at that."

"What the hell is going on, Admiral?" I almost screamed into the phone. "It was a major incident. A bomb went off right on a US Navy base."

"I don't think it's in the IRA's interest to cause harm to an American base or its people," Admiral Schmidt said. "After all, much funding for the Catholic insurgents comes from the States. A few years ago, they were after weapons from the armory. In my opinion, this recent bombing was to put you in your place, to let you know they can get inside the base and cause serious damage."

"I think the Catholic insurgents or the Protestants are warning us about turning the base over to the British Army," I said. "Our plan to do this sounds more and more dangerous each day."

"That may be so," said Admiral Schmidt, "but this doesn't change your mission."

A few seconds of silence followed.

"Be careful how you word your report," Admiral Schmidt said. "We'll send someone to evaluate your security. Maybe get a few more arms on the base."

"A few more arms?" I said in disbelief. "I need more than arms. I need marines who know how to use the arms."

"That is all, Captain McKeown," said Admiral Schmidt, and the phone went dead.

I was breathing heavily, like someone who had just run a race. My heart was beating hard, and there was sweat rolling down my face.

I spent the rest of the day assessing the damage and trying to figure out what happened and why. A few hours after the blast, Bob McManus came in and said the bomb had come in on a bicycle that was parked near the gym.

"It looks like it was a plastic bomb left next to the gymnasium," said Bob. "Hidden in the basket of a bicycle and set off remotely. I've got some navy witnesses who saw a civilian riding a bike near the gym about twenty minutes before the explosion."

"But the guards at the front gate never saw the bike?" I asked.

"No," said McManus. "No one is sure how it got on the base. We're continuing to investigate the incident and are interviewing a number of people. There were no injuries, and the damage to the gym was mainly a few blown-out windows and some scars on the outside of the building but no structural damage."

"Call a meeting with all my senior staff tomorrow morning," I said. "Nine o'clock."

"Will do, Captain," Bob said.

I spent the rest of the afternoon writing up my report of the "event" on the base. I knew it was futile to tell the truth of the event. It would only be covered up to avoid US and British media publication. Around six, Moira poked her head into the office and told me she was going home if I didn't need her.

"No, go ahead and go home," I said.

It was early evening, and I was the only one in the office. I stood at the window of my office that looked east down the hill and toward Londonderry a few miles in the distance. Patches of clouds hung over the town, but here and there, parts of Londonderry were highlighted by streaks of sunlight coming through the clouds. The top spire of St. Columb's Cathedral was gold from the light of the afternoon sun, and behind the cathedral, in the distance, the Bogside area of town was bathed in afternoon sunlight like a benediction at the end of this difficult day.

I turned off the light in the office and was getting ready to go home when the phone rang. After the emotional stress from the day, the jingle of my desk phone startled me. Thinking it was one of my officers, I grabbed it quickly.

"Captain McKeown," a deep, raspy Irish voice growled in almost a murmur.

"Who is this?" I demanded.

"Me name doesn't matter much these days," the voice said. "Just let it be said that we wanted to give ye a small bit of a taste of what might be happening to the entire navy base should ye get the notion to turn it over to the stinkin', bloody army."

I listened with disbelief.

"Now, I know yer gonna tell me it's the queen's decision, but ta hell with her," the voice said. "We'll crush and burn yer base ta ashes and all in it, including yer family. Now is that clear enough ta ye, Captain?"

No discussion was possible with this voice. This somehow seemed obvious at the time to me.

"I heard you," I said.

There was no answer on the phone but only a click. After the call, I sat in my office with the lights off, trying to figure out what to do. It was bad enough that I might be in danger, but I hated the threat against my family.

I seemed caught in a no-win game. I was moved by the stories I had heard from civilian employees that day. Yes, the bartender in the Donegal pub got it right. I was little more than a hatchet man, here to do the navy's dirty work of closing down a beloved facility and putting many families out on the streets. As a navy man, I was never much fond of the army anyway, British or American. *This is crazy*, I thought.

At the same time, I was a loyal officer in the US Navy with a mission ordered by the president himself.

Things were becoming more complicated, and it was getting difficult to separate the heroes from the villains in this crazy affair and even more difficult to determine which side I wanted to be on in the first place. In all of my missions before, religion never played much of a role in things. It was always there, in the background, but it never was like some flag to rally behind in a war. Now, though, it seemed such an essential piece of the whole puzzle. I couldn't forget the feeling

I had last week when I saw the "Free Derry" sign for the first time. The emotions it brought forth still swirled about inside me like some homeless spirit.

The phone rang again, and the noise made me jump.

I moved toward it, wondering what message it would bring this time. I slowly picked it up.

"We're worried about you," said Mary. "When are you coming home?"

Relief came over my body.

"On my way," I said.

Chapter 13

Dealing with Reality

Darkness had fallen when I walked home from my office. I wondered how Mary would be with the news of the bombing. A guard stood in front of my home and saluted as I walked past him and into the house.

The children came running toward me and gave me hugs. Tara was clutching her hobbit.

"Daddy, there's a man in front of our house," she said.

"Yes, I know," I replied. "He is there to make sure all of our family is OK."

"Are you OK, Dad?" Shawn asked. "We heard the explosion. Is that blood on your shirt?"

"I'm fine," I said. "A piece of glass cut my neck, but the corpsman fixed me up. No one was seriously injured."

"A couple guys told me it was the IRA," Shawn continued. "Is that so?"

"We don't know yet. We're still trying to find out." I knew that I could not tell them about my strange call and my suspicion was the IRA or the Orangemen were behind the bombing.

"Everyone off to bed," said Mary, approaching out of the kitchen, holding two glasses of wine. "Your father and I need to talk."

The children wanted to stay up and hear about the bomb, but Mary was adamant that they go to bed. They kissed Mary and me good night and were gone. Tara told me that she asked the hobbit to put a special magic protection over our home, and the hobbit said he would. When the children were gone, Mary and I went out into the backyard and sat in the comfy chairs in the garden.

It was a dark night with thick clouds overhead that hid the moonlight. The lights of Londonderry twinkled a few miles away, but they seemed dimmer tonight than they had in the past, little more than a congregation of dying lightning bugs that had fallen out of the sky.

Mary looked up at the clouds.

"No, northern lights tonight," she said.

"They're still there. You just can't see them."

"Maybe, but maybe they're gone."

"They're not going anywhere. They've been here for a million years, and they'll be here for another million years."

"Things seem so different now than a month ago when we first got here."

"Things change."

"I wish they didn't change."

"That's an impossible wish."

"I thought things were changing for us."

"They are changing."

"It's nice to have you home, but you said there was little or no danger in coming over here. You knew it was much more dangerous than you told us. You were willing to put your family in danger for your own selfish interests."

This was like a dagger in my heart!

"Is it selfish to want my family with me?" I shot back.

"Yes, if it's in the middle of a war!"

"It's not our war."

"It's still a war, and we're in the middle of it."

"The Irish love us Americans."

"Tell that to me after something happens to one of the children."

"Nothing is going to happen to the children. Besides, Tara's hobbit is protecting us."

"Don't be ridiculous."

"Maybe you just have to believe in things a little more. After all, we're in the land of hobbits and magic."

"Maybe I've believed in something too long."

We sat in silence in the backyard for a few moments.

"You know I love you," Mary said. "But I'm scared."

She kissed me on my hand, and then she went back into the house.

I sat in the yard and poured another glass of wine. Should I go inside and tell Mary the real fate of the base and make her a confidante in the secret plan? God knows I need a confidante these days. But I decided against it. Telling her this would only make her more worried.

It was like telling someone on board a ship they were headed into a group of icebergs and there was nothing to do to stop the ship.

Chapter 14

Base Operations

At nine o'clock the next morning, the office conference room was packed with senior staff members. I stood at the end of the table and could see uneasiness and fright in the eyes of my officers. Stress was evident in their faces and postures. I guessed they were wondering how their new commanding officer was going to react to the bombing incident. Certainly, they were now more concerned about their safety.

"Good morning," I said. "Of all the navy commands I've been fortunate to be given, I've never received such an 'explosively' warm greeting. Even in Vietnam, it took at least a month before someone tried to shoot me."

My attempt at humor fell on blast-deafened ears, although a few in the room managed a weak smile.

"Ladies and gentlemen," I continued, "yesterday, the Irish Gardaí, British Army, and our naval officers pretty much concluded that the bombing event was a warning to us by the Provisional IRA or the Orangemen not to turn this base over to the British Army." *It seemed coincidental as Ian Nelson, an Orangeman was speaking, but I didn't want to accuse him during the meeting.* "Fortunately, none of our people were seriously injured. Cuts and bruises, yes, and scared, but most of us came back to work today. Even though the US Navy loves this base and needs this base to support the fleet, we've been given orders to close it because of the surrounding danger to our personnel."

A noticeable stir, with shifting about in chairs and mumbling, swept over the gathering.

"The president and the secretary of defense do not want any of our military, their families, or our civilian employees to be harmed. Other than the attempted robbery of the armory and the destruction of the microwave towers, yesterday's event was the first time anyone was injured. Although there were a few minor injuries, we believe it was not their intention to hurt anyone. Just to frighten us. And that they did."

I paused and tried to make eye contact with as many as possible in a few seconds.

"Are there any questions?" I asked.

Chief Warrant Officer Jim Emberton stood up. "Captain, do you think they'll do it again?"

After sucking in my breath, I responded, "I don't think so. I think it was meant as a warning. I'm the new guy on the block. I'm the hatchet man, the closer. I must make one point clear to all of you. We are *not* giving this base to the British Army, no matter what you may hear. We are returning the property to the queen, to the United Kingdom."

Trying to manage a hopeful, enthusiastic smile, I added, "And at the same time, and this is new to you, we are going to gradually transfer our mission and operational responsibilities to the naval communications facility in Thurso, Scotland. Soon, we will receive orders as to the disposition of functions and property. Until then, I want to remind you of a few critical security matters. First, I've asked for marines to come to our base and give us some security recommendations. Next, remember the people of Derry love Americans. So, whenever you or anyone in your family enters a store or a pub in this town, always say and do whatever it takes to make it obvious that you are an American. If you have an accent, use it early on as you enter the premises, loud and clear. Wear clothes that look American. Communicate this to the sailors under your command."

Glancing over the audience, I could see that there was great attention to what I had just told them. Certainly it was important they understood what was being said.

"I want to emphasize again that no one on either side of the troubles wants to hurt an American. And why is this? Because neither side wants to jeopardize the monetary support, weapons, and political support that are coming from America. Finally, we are also doubling up the guards around the perimeter of the base, making sure the gate guards are more careful as to who enters the base, and most important of all, we are having our school buses escorted to and from the off-base schools by the British Army. I have also asked for a marine detachment to train our sailors in the use of firearms."

The next month on the base came and went without incident, but now fear was added to the anxiety of the base closing. There was a new caution in everyday life, a suspicion of people. A number of sailors were reassigned to guard duty, and more arms were somehow squeezed out of the Pentagon for the base. Vehicles coming and going from the base were searched more thoroughly than ever before.

Gradually, things returned to a certain degree of normalcy. There was still important work to be done; ships and submarines remained out on the sea and depended on us for support. Until the base in Thurso, Scotland, was up and running, Londonderry was still the main communications station for the US Navy in the North Atlantic.

The primary function of the base was communications, reception, and transmission, and the associated equipment was operated by radiomen and maintained by electronics technicians. The remaining base departments were for logistics and maintenance. Numerous jobs were performed by civilians, mostly local employees.

The heart of operations was on the main base at the communications center. The Receivers site was located in an open field full of vast antennas. Twenty miles away in Dungiven was the transmitter site. All of them were in operation twenty-four hours a day. Because of the latitude of Londonderry, during the summer, it wouldn't get dark until late in the night, and during the winter, it would get dark around 3:00 p.m. Depending on their shift, the sailors might not see the sun or the moon for a couple of days.

Chapter 15

Life on the Base

I felt sports were important as a way of boosting the morale on the base. I made sure that there were sufficient athletic events for the sailors and families on the base. I boosted the program of bringing local athletic clubs from Londonderry to the base to play various sports or taking base teams off the base to play local Irish teams.

The base basketball team was decent, usually holding its own against most of the other teams in Northern Ireland. The baseball team always excelled, since the locals were mostly new to the game. But the glaring problem was the base soccer team in the sport that defined everyone in Northern Ireland, like football defined things in America. As Jimmy told me, the base soccer team sucked.

I had made a note of the world-class soccer coach, Charlie Wilson, whom Jimmy had mentioned while on the tour of the base. I called Charlie and met with him. We worked out an agreement for Charlie to coach the base soccer team. He had been a star high school player and coach before joining the navy. The team was startled and pleased that he was one of ours and a chief master-at-arms. It was hard to believe that he was going to be our new coach.

Besides sports, I did a number of other things to help boost morale on the base during these difficult times. I revitalized the social committee on the base and brought some top local rock bands onto the base for a number of events at Sampson Hall. I activated a number of base clubs and began republishing the old base newsletter the *Mr. Edhorn*.

George O'Donnell was my advisor in much of my efforts to restore morale. I had heard stories from George of how the base used to be—their championship sports teams, their great social functions, the community they had back in the forties and fifties—so I did not try to implement new programs but simply bring back old ones that had begun to shut down with knowledge of the base closing in everyone's minds.

It was impossible to find hot dogs or bologna anywhere in Northern Ireland or in the republic. Consequently, a smuggling operation developed on the base during this time. It involved Mother's Pride bread, which was like gold in London. Some of the guys in the kitchen traded cases of bread for cases of bologna until their London "source" was transferred back to the States. They tried their best to get bologna for their desperate cravings but had no luck until someone happened to remember a brother who was a butcher and had a recipe for bologna. They had this sacred recipe transferred to a butcher in Londonderry, and he kept them happy with makeshift bologna and hot dogs until the IRA blew up his local shop in Derry.

The enlisted club (EC) was frequented more often, and the sailors got back to their old pranks. One night at the EC, a number of sailors were drinking, celebrating one of them getting married. The subject of blackening came up. Blackening was a strange Scottish tradition of stripping the groom to the waist and covering his torso with some black substance, like shoe polish.

So they decided to carry on that bit of tradition right then and there and stripped the shirt off the new groom. But they didn't stop with just a bare chest. They decided it would be better if he was totally naked and stripped off all of his clothes. Then, they threw him into the chief's club, where there was a formal event underway. After this, they ran his clothes up the base flagpole, where I saw them flying on my way to the office the next morning. I wasn't happy about this, and I called the base master chief and let him know. However, I did call the prospective groom into my office and congratulate him.

⌐╗╙

Things were difficult with Mary, and it was impossible for me to read her mind as to whether she was going to leave with the children or stay. The explosion had almost been the final straw for her. Almost. Gradually, she got involved with some of the wives' groups, like the book club, Meals on Wheels, and the bowling league. She and the children began to establish friendships, and the days started to pass faster and faster. At first, the women's bowling club was just enlisted wives, and the language was free and easy. The bowling alley was on the second floor of Sampson Hall. The women would call the EC, which was right next door, for drinks, and one of the bartenders would bring them over.

When the skipper's wife joined, there was a feeling of doom and gloom as they would have to be on their best behavior all the time. There was tension the first time Mary showed up to bowl with the group. But when she threw a gutter ball, she exclaimed, "Oh shit!" This broke the ice, and the happy, relaxed atmosphere returned. She became a popular member of the club.

I watched this slow transformation with my wife. Perhaps our marriage might make it after all and Mary would not leave me and go back to the States. Perhaps that old fire of so many years ago might be rekindled. Things were looking up with Mary, but it was still too early to tell.

As there was no equivalent American high school for Shawn to attend in Londonderry, he was sent to room and board at the Department of Defense High School in High Wychum, England. We hated to see him leave, but at his age, we knew it was the best thing for him, not only for his education, but to keep him safe from the violence in Northern Ireland. We would see him every few months and on holidays.

⌒⌒⌒

I wanted to confide in Mary about the real ending of the base. Holding all of this inside was one of the most difficult things I had ever done.

Returning the base and its property to the queen was too heavy to bear alone. I needed a confidante. I thought of telling her a number of times. But I sensed it was a bad idea. She had enough on her mind, trying to cope with the new surroundings, being the captain's wife, and helping the new wives and mothers she was getting to know.

In addition, I became aware that Sunday Catholic services were void on the base. I mentioned this to my executive officer. He was flabbergasted and shocked that we had never had a Catholic Mass on base.

"Do we have a chapel on the base?"

"Yes, sir. We have a small chapel behind the communications center, where the men occasionally gather to pray."

"Is there a Catholic church in Derry?"

"There may be one that hasn't been blown up yet. I don't know."

"Then I will personally take on the job."

I called Jimmy Emberton to get the jeep, and we drove into town. After quite a jaunt throughout the city, we came upon Our Lady of Sorrow, a small brick building with most of the windows blown out and the door ajar, as the hinges were missing. The priest, a young fellow, was kneeling by the altar, which had been stripped of its tabernacle. We quietly entered the church and walked toward the altar. I put my hand on the priest's shoulder. He jumped in fear.

"Oh my heavens, ye startled me."

I introduced myself.

He, in turn, replied, "I am Father John Mullins, sir."

The three of us sat in a pew that was covered with dust and debris.

"Father, I would like you to come to my base and conduct Mass for the sailors."

Father Mullins looked at me with a puzzled expression.

"Father, I will get you an organ and vestments and whatever else you need. I can assure you that you will be safe while on the base. I know there are many Catholic men and women on my base who will be delighted to assist you."

Jimmy also assured the father that he would get sailors to escort him to and from the town. Looking at both of us, Father agreed.

"And when would you like me to come?"

Jimmy replied, "Father, I will pick you up at eight hundred this Sunday morning."

"And what time is that?" asked Father Mullins.

"Eight in the morning," Jimmy replied.

Chapter 16

The Town of Derry

Things settled down on the base after the explosion, but the violence continued in Londonderry and Northern Ireland with sectarian shootings, IRA and UVA/UVF bombings, checkpoints, armored vehicles, helicopter patrols, and soldiers with machine guns everywhere. Even our Irish relatives in Sligo and County Mayo refused to come and visit us because they were afraid to cross the border into Northern Ireland.

On September 4, 1976, there was a Peace People's rally in Derry that was attended by approximately 2,500 people. And during the following weeks, there were a number of rallies all over Ireland and Britain. There was a bomb scare at the train station across the street from the Waterside School in Londonderry, and the base children were then sent to Maydown near the DuPont plant. I provided a navy bus, but the parents had to provide the drivers, so a number of them made the effort to get qualified to drive a school bus. The school bus was escorted by two guard jeeps—one in front and one in back.

From the base, you could hear bombs going off at all hours of the day. Across Clooney Road from the base was a place called the Broomhill Hotel. Those on the base used to call it the Boomhill, because it seemed to attract the attention of the IRA. Those who lived on the side of the base nearest the hotel would often get a call to open their windows and take things off the walls whenever there was a bomb threat at the Boomhill. Opening the windows would save one from injuries caused by flying glass, and it would also save public works from replacing the windows.

Things were extremely tense in downtown Londonderry. A few wives went downtown one day and had to stop at a checkpoint. As the British soldiers looked through the purse of one of the women, the women were ordered up against a wall with guns pointed at them. One of the women's children had put his cap pistol in his mother's purse, and it looked like a real gun at first glance. The soldiers discovered the toy gun and released the women.

⌒〟〟⌒

One day, a guard from the gatehouse knocked on the door of my home, and Mary answered.

It was Willy McGafferty, who was somewhere in his seventies and ready to retire after being a guard for thirty years.

"Just wondering when Shawn will be back from school in England," he said.

Shawn had developed a friendship with the old man, who took him around the base and showed him secret places like ponds and creeks, hidden caves, and this old abandoned tree house in one corner. He also gave Shawn an old quarter horse that grazed in the fields behind the transmitter site.

"He'll be home in a month for the holidays," Mary said. "I'm sure he wants to see you."

"We've got a little gift for him," the old man said.

"That's wonderful," said Mary. "So thoughtful of you."

Mary could see that there was something else on the old man's mind.

"Care to come in for a spot of tea?" she asked.

"Don't mind if I do."

He followed her into the kitchen, and she put on a pot of tea and offered him some cookies. He took a few and thanked her. As she poured him a cup of tea, she noticed he was staring at the bottle of Jameson Irish whiskey on the shelf of the kitchen. A streak of morning sunlight was coming through the kitchen window, illuminating in gold the bottle of Jameson so that it almost looked like a religious object. Mary could see that Willy was staring at the bottle.

"Perhaps you'd like me to freshen up the tea?" she said, reaching for the bottle of Jameson.

At first, he said he shouldn't, but then he said that one small dab of Jameson was good for the soul. Mary poured the Jameson into his tea, and the old man drank it down in one quick gulp.

"Awfully nice of you, Mrs. McKeown," the large Irishman said as he got up to leave.

Right before he went out the door, he turned to her.

"Be wise to stay away from Austin's department store tomorrow," Willy said.

The department store in downtown Londonderry was the world's oldest independent department store, and a lot of people on the base shopped there for all sorts of things.

"Why is that?" Mary asked.

"Just wise to avoid it tomorrow," Willy said. "If ye know what I mean."

Then he was gone—back to his duty at the gatehouse. As soon as Willy had departed, Mary called me at the office and informed me of the pending danger. I immediately ordered all department heads to notify their people to avoid Austin's the following day.

The next afternoon, there was the sound of a major explosion in downtown Derry. A bomb went off at Austin's, and hundreds of people were killed and injured, but luckily, all base personnel were unharmed.

Willy soon became a regular caller at our home for his daily shot of Jameson or to deliver a word of warning, sometimes both. After several weeks of Willy's warnings becoming reality, Mary suggested that perhaps Willy might be connected to the Provisional IRA.

I was not surprised. "Every civilian employee up here is connected to the IRA or the Protestants in some way. Just keep him coming over for the Jameson's. His information is valuable no matter where it comes from."

So Mary made a point to let Willy know that he was always welcome to stop over at the house for a short nip of Jameson's and should he have any worthwhile information, it would be appreciated. I made it my job to keep a full supply of Jameson's on hand.

The old guard began to trudge over to my home on a regular basis, and Mary became a type of early warning system for bombings in Londonderry. Almost all the times Willy said there was going to be an incident, something happened, and it got to the point where people would call Mary before going downtown.

There were checkpoints all over the town, where you were stopped and checked by British troops. Often, you were searched before going into any stores or pubs in town.

One day, Jimmy Emberton headed downtown in his old jalopy, wearing his Tennessee ball cap and shiny cowboy boots with elaborate designs in the leather. He was driving across the bridge into town. The Brits had a checkpoint in the middle of the bridge. As he stopped at the checkpoint, two British soldiers asked him if they could look inside his "boot."

Jimmy said sure and opened the door, spun around in his seat, and proceeded to pull off one of his shiny boots. The demeanor of the British soldier changed instantly.

"Quit being a smart-ass, Yank," he said. "Back there," he said, motioning with his head toward the back of the car.

So Jimmy went to the back of his car, leaned on the trunk, and started to bend over to take off his boots. At this time, they realized he didn't know the English meaning of "boot" was the trunk of a car and not a shoe. The two British troops had a good laugh at this and waved him through the checkpoint. And Jimmy learned a new English word.

A few new electronic technicians on the base told the story at the EC one night about walking in downtown Londonderry on one side of the street as a British squad was walking single file on the other side. The squad came to a halt, and the last soldier walking backward spotted the ET guys and pointed his gun at them. A few seconds later, the squad started to advance, and the soldier put his rifle down. They proceeded down the street. A sailor who had been on the base for a year told them that they must have looked suspicious and that the British soldier was using the scope on his rifle to get a close-up look at their faces.

"The Brits can usually tell the Americans by what they wear," the experienced sailor told them. "Blue jeans and white tennis shoes are good things to wear downtown. It's also a good thing to speak up using your native accent when you enter the pubs so they know you're a Yank."

⌐⊅⊓⊓⊳

I got to be good friends with George O'Donnell, my senior civilian of the base, and Warrant Officer Jimmy Emberton. George was somewhat of a mentor to us, as his thirty years on the base allowed him to provide a broader perspective on things. And Jimmy became my sidekick and golfing buddy during a number of weekend golf outings to the famous Portrush golf course on the northwest coast.

One evening, when the northern lights were putting on a spectacular display over the base, the three of us drove into town to have a few pints at the Clarendon pub on Strand Road in downtown Derry. The red and black building near the River Foyle was one of our favorite American hangouts and was a safe place to wind down from a day on the base. It was getting late, and the place was thinning out. There were a few guys at the bar, and a dart game was in progress. Talk turned to the danger to the base from the IRA. Despite the ongoing violence around the base, there had been no more incidents on the base.

"I doubt if the IRA would ever attack the base," Jimmy said. "They love the Americans too much."

George O'Donnell smiled and shook his head in disagreement.

"That's where you're wrong, lad," he said. "They might love you Americans, but they don't love you as much as they hate the British."

I pondered the simple, logical wisdom of the native civilian who had been on the base longer than anyone else.

"You really think the IRA will attack the base again?" I asked George.

The old Irishman looked into his Guinness and swirled it around like it was a liquid black crystal ball.

"Of course they will if they think the base will be handed over to the British Army," he said.

"It's a good thing we're turning the base over to the queen," Jimmy said.

Jimmy's words hung in the thick, smoky air of the pub without comment. Some Irish tune made background music over the boisterous sound of the dart game and a few old guys telling stories at the bar.

I didn't say anything. I suspected George somehow knew about the plan to turn the base over to the British Army. Why wouldn't he know? He knew everything else going on at the base. It was not too much to suspect he also knew this. In the darkness of the pub, I thought I could detect a quick wink from George O'Donnell, but it was difficult to know for sure.

George raised his pint of Guinness at Jimmy.

"Yes, Jimmy," George said. "A good thing indeed."

On the drive back to the base, the town of Derry looked ominous and forbidding to me. A few people on the street morphed into potential terrorists. I was sure that the car behind was following us. The short backfires of a passing motorcycle seemed like gunshots and made me jerk.

And overhead, the northern lights had lost their beauty and now seemed like the threatening explosions of some advancing force of the IRA moving toward the base, ready to create havoc and preventing the base from being turned over to the British Army.

Yes, I thought about George's comment, like so many things in life, it all comes down to the matter of love and hate. Love was a powerful emotion, and there was such a long history between the Americans and the town of Londonderry. But hate was an even more powerful emotion with a much longer history.

In Londonderry, the love between the Americans and the citizens of Derry was thirty-five years old. But the hate between the Catholics and British went on for centuries, as old as the Irish legends, as perpetual as the northern lights. A perpetual, legendary hate.

Chapter 17

Closing Preparations

The summer slowly moved into the past, and autumn came to Northern Ireland, bringing afternoon darkness, more rain, and cooler days but no change in the bombings and violence throughout the city. The base being so near the downtown area of Londonderry, there was the constant sound of explosions and gunfire, and this became a steady background Muzak to life on the base, as persistent as the hum of communications from the big antennas.

I worked to keep everything on a steady course toward closing the base down, but the transition program continued to move slowly in Thurso, Scotland. There were delays in getting permits and delays in getting materials. I decided to fly to Scotland and meet with people over there to see if the base could be opened sooner and communications transferred. Until Thurso was ready, there was no way the Londonderry base could shut down. It was critical for navy communications.

I asked Jimmy to go with me and be sure to take his golf clubs. We were going to the birthplace of golf, and I had plans to play the famous St. Andrews course over there if time would allow.

***

I didn't say much about the trip, and speculation about its purpose became a hot topic at the EM club and the officer's club. It particularly concerned George O'Donnell, who called a meeting at the Bogside flat of Sean and Shannon Kelly to discuss things.

Late one evening, a group of IRA leaders in Londonderry sat around the kitchen table in the small flat over bottles of Guinness. Willy McGafferty was one of the people at the table nursing a tall glass of Jameson.

Shannon Kelly said it was impossible to know the purpose of my trip to Scotland other than to meet with some people on the base and play golf. As Moira's assistant to me in the base office, she had the best perspective to know what was going on. But she couldn't make out what the trip to Scotland meant.

"The plans to turn the base over to the British Army haven't changed," George O'Donnell said. "This I'm sure of. The only question is when."

"Maybe the purpose of the captain's trip to Scotland is to speed things up," Sean Kelly offered.

"Perhaps," said George.

"If that's so, we need to operate quickly," Sean said.

"Aye," George replied. "Ye could be right."

"When will we know?" asked Sean Kelly.

"We might never know," said George. "We might have to just take action before the base closes down."

"We're ready for your orders to start destructive action," Sean said to George.

"Let's wait a little longer," George said. "For the first time, we've got an Irish Catholic running things on the base. I have a modicum of faith that something might happen to change things."

"Aye, you have more faith than I do," said Sean.

"I know the captain better than you do," replied George.

"So we'll give it a little more time before we take any negative action against the Derry base. We do not want the British Army to take over this property. If they do, they will have nothing but rubble. That's right, a little more time."

Before the meeting was over, George O'Donnell gave Willy McGafferty a sheet of paper.

"See these dates and places? Get them to Mary McKeown," George said. "We have no desire to have anyone from the base harmed."

⌒⌇⌒

Thurso, Scotland, was a small town of a few thousand people on the northeastern tip of Scotland, the most northern town in all of the United Kingdom. Jimmy drove down to St. Andrews to make arrangements to play the famous old course. One had to put one's name on what was called a lottery to play the course. I spent a day on the base in Thurso, meeting with senior staff.

In my meetings, I heard of numerous problems they were having expanding the base. There were many permit problems with endless Scottish regulations to be observed and problems getting new equipment on the base. I sensed something was not right but couldn't put my finger on it.

Right before I left, Lieutenant Erick Roberts, executive officer on the base, came up to me and asked if I wanted to grab a pint.

"Of course," I said.

Erick Roberts was a two-striper who had been shifted to Thurso from some operations jobs at various navy bases. His last assignment was at the big navy base in San Diego. He was a blond California kid in his late twenties and was as far from San Diego as you could go.

After a few pints, Lieutenant Roberts loosened up a little. He quickly glanced around the pub and then leaned across the table toward me.

"I might not know much about Scotland, Captain," he said, "but I know a little about base operations. Things just don't add up."

"How so?" I inquired.

"The base is costing a lot more money than anyone anticipated. We've already gone way over budget, and we're still months away from expanding."

"The navy has been known to underestimate things before," I said. "I can tell you this firsthand."

"But this is the first time I've been ordered not to report all the operating expenses."

"Ordered by who?" I demanded.

"By the American embassy in London."

"Who at the embassy?"

"Some senior staff member for the ambassador."

"Who?"

"I don't know. He is given a code name, and you know how hard it is to get behind code names."

I didn't say anything but just looked into my pint of Guinness.

"Orders are coming from someone working for the ambassador to cover up expenses of expanding Thurso," Roberts said. "I shouldn't be telling you this, sir," he continued. "But since I'm going to be working for you in a few months, I—"

I interrupted. "Have you told this to anyone else?"

"Who could I tell, sir?"

"You've got documentation of the true operating costs of the base?" I asked.

"My own figures," said Roberts. "I started tracking them myself when I saw things that didn't make any sense. They're back at the office."

"I need a copy of what you have."

"Captain, I can get in some deep—"

"That's an order, Lieutenant," I said.

We drove back to his office on the new base, and he unlocked a file and pulled out two notebooks.

"The real operating figures are in this book, and mine are in this book," he said, handing the notebooks to me. "The figures from the ambassador's office and my own figures for Thurso expenses."

"I need copies of these notebooks," I said.

Lieutenant Roberts made copies of the contents of both notebooks, punched holes in them, and put them into two new notebooks. He handed them to me.

"What's all this mean, Captain?" he asked.

"Hard to tell."

"What should I do?"

"Nothing right now. Just continue doing what you've been ordered to do by Washington and me. I want you to keep me informed on a daily basis as to the progress of expanding the base, including communication sites and new housing. I will be making a trip to Thurso at least every two to three weeks."

I thought about what Lieutenant Roberts had told me on our drive back to my hotel in downtown Thurso. I stopped in the pub for one final pint before going to bed. Jimmy Emberton was already there.

"Jimmy, I plan to move you and your family to Thurso early so that you can look over financial expenditures there."

"Yes Sir" Jimmy replied. "This will make my wife happy. She's from Scotland, ya know Captain."

I knew that nothing was finished with the Thurso base and that it was only the beginning of something I would have to look into when

I got back to Londonderry. It was another piece of information to be tucked away somewhere.

The next day, Jimmy and I drove to the famous Royal Dornoch Golf Club. We arrived early for our tee time. The course was everything both of us had heard about it—austere, beautiful, magnificent.

We parked the navy car, put our golf shoes on, and walked to the small round starter's shack.

"Can I help ye gentlemen?" said a bifocaled elderly man in his rapid Scottish speech.

"Of course," Jimmy replied in his southern drawl. "This here's my US Navy captain."

The elderly man was not impressed. "What's the name?" he asked. "It doesn't matter if he is a captain."

The old Scotsman summoned two caddies, who followed Jimmy to the car where the clubs were, and we four were off to the first tee.

"We don't have a golf cart?" I asked.

The caddies smiled at each other with toothy grins.

"No buggies at this course, sir," one of them said. "We're all yer gonna get."

"All right," Jimmy said. "Let's get going on this here course."

I had played many golf courses in my life, but this one was special. It was the type of golf course one played once in a lifetime if one was lucky enough.

"By the way," Jimmy said to the caddies after a few holes, "have you boys ever had a nip of American Jack Daniels?"

The caddies smiled and shook their heads.

"Now that ye ask, sir," one of them said, "that's a pleasure we haven't tasted."

"Well," Jimmy said, "you are all welcome anytime to this here bottle in my golf bag. Just let me know."

Jimmy took the bottle of Jack Daniels from his golf bag.

"Might use a nip right now," one of the caddies said.

Jimmy passed the bottle to him, and he took a long drink and smiled approvingly. Then he passed it to the other caddy, who also took a long drink and smiled.

"Ye have a mighty fine whiskey," one of the caddies said.

The golf game was the most fun and the most thrilling one we ever experienced. The two old caddies continued to take "nips" at the bottle of Jack Daniels during the round and never stopped talking, giving advice on how to play the holes and telling stories of the many famous professionals they had worked for. As we went down the eighteenth fairway, they finished off the bottle of Jack Daniels and Jimmy and I had to help the old boys carry the golf bags.

We flew back to Northern Ireland that evening. Jimmy talked excitedly about the incredible Dornoch course and the clubhouse with all the hickory clubs and feathered golf balls. I smiled as I listened to Jimmy recap the incredible day. It was one of the best days in my life.

But my talk at the pub with Lieutenant Roberts was on my mind. I looked out the airplane window into the darkness, wondering what my next move should be. Something was not right with the way things were going at Thurso. The notebook with all the figures Roberts gave me was in my briefcase. I would have to go through it when I got back to the base.

⌐⁊⫘⫘

When I got back to Londonderry, I called the ambassador's office in London and asked to speak to the ambassador. I got a promise that the ambassador would get back to me later. I needed to get to the bottom of the two sets of figures for Thurso. A week passed, and I called the ambassador's office back when I didn't hear from him. I was told the ambassador was still away but would call me when he arrived back in the office. I thought about calling Admiral Schmidt in Washington on the matter, but I felt it best to talk to the ambassador first before coming to any conclusions. There might be an explanation for the whole thing that Lieutenant Roberts was not privy to. I was not about to call the admiral until I had talked to the ambassador.

The question of Thurso expenses became lost in all of the hundreds of daily tasks of running the Londonderry base as well as transferring responsibilities to Thurso. It was becoming obvious to me that proper oversight was not being carried out as far as expanding operations and expenditures matching build-out projects. I came to the conclusion that this was just poor financial accounting and Jimmy Emberton would clear it up.

Chapter 18

Everyday Living with Terror

October brought a number of parades and festivities in Londonderry. The IRA paraded through town, wearing masks over their faces like they always did. It was not a good idea for people to know who members of the IRA were. There was another parade of the Protestant Orangemen through town, wearing their black suits, bowler hats, and orange sashes across their shoulders. When they marched through the Catholic sections of town, little children tossed stones at their bowler hats, trying to knock them off their heads. It was a game that had been played for many years.

Ian Nelson watched the marchers go by from the crowded sidewalk and took off his black bowler hat as the Orange Order flag passed. He would be marching with them, but it was not wise to advertise he was an Orangeman with his position on the navy base.

Shawn got a week off from school in High Wychum and flew back to Northern Ireland. Mary told him that Willy McGafferty had a special gift for him, and Shawn excitedly ran over to the guardhouse to see what it was.

He returned home half an hour later, riding bareback on an old gray horse that looked like it was on its last legs.

"Look what Willy gave me!" he excitedly told his mom. "Meet Mr. Ed."

Mary was startled to see Shawn on the horse.

"What are you ever going to do with Mr. Ed?" she asked.

"Willy says I can keep Mr. Ed up in the antenna field if it's OK with Dad—be a good place for him."

I was surprised to see the horse when I got home but told Shawn that it would be OK to keep Mr. Ed in the antenna field if he was properly fed and tied up. Shawn agreed to this, and he went off to discuss the logistics of all of this with Willy.

Shawn rode Mr. Ed bareback all around the base, wearing an Indian outfit we had given him. The base guards helped him take food up to the antenna field for Mr. Ed and made sure he was securely tied to one of the radio towers.

But when Shawn went back to school in High Wychum, there was less supervision of Mr. Ed, and one day, the old gray horse chewed his way through the ropes tied to the radio tower and ran off the base, down the hill, over the bridge, and through the streets of Londonderry. Jimmy and a number of people from the base came into town to try to catch him, and even some British soldiers got into the chase, which took everyone past the St. Columb Cathedral and all the way into the Bogside area of town.

I was in a meeting with my officers when Moira entered the meeting room and said, "Excuse me, Captain, but your son's horse was running around town and was being chased by the British Army and the Bobbies, but he was finally caught not too far from the Free Derry wall."

Mr. Ed soon became a familiar member of the family. One morning, as I was lying in bed coping with a slight hangover, Mr. Ed's old gray face was looking at me with his head in the window, showing all his teeth. I yelled for Mary. She and the kids came running to the bedroom and started to laugh. Mary took one look at Mr. Ed and soon realized he had just enjoyed the bowl of Korean kimchi she had placed on the table in the backyard to age. Colleen quickly filled a bucket full of water and offered it to Mr. Ed.

⌒⌒

The base soccer team continued to improve under Coach Chief Wilson. They made a giant leap forward when the team joined the Saturday Morning D & D League, comprising teams far more advanced than they were. The competiveness and enthusiasm dramatically increased, and the team got better and actually won a match and then another. People started gathering to watch them play, and there were some write-ups about them in the local paper.

⌒⌒

In good faith, George O'Donnell gave Willy a week's worth of planned terrorist attacks to be passed on to Mary. Of course, this was the way that Willy was able to warn Mary during his daily morning nip. Unfortunately, Willy lost the list one evening while drinking at his favorite Derry pub. The list was addressed to Willy. Ironically, the list found its way to the hierarchy of the IRA. The list compromised the whole week of destructive activity. Early one morning, before reveille, a terrible crash was heard throughout the base. The sound of crunching metal and breaking glass resonated everywhere. I quickly put on my trousers and ran toward the gate, along with many other concerned folks. A huge, heavy dump truck had careened through the gate and smashed into the guardhouse. Willy McGafferty was on duty. The crowd began searching frantically for Willy and calling his name. The truck driver was nowhere in sight.

I shouted, "Go get the corpsman!"

My XO, Bob McManus, said, "Captain, it's too late. Willy is dead."

At that moment, Mary arrived at the guardhouse and realized Willy was gone. She began to weep uncontrollably. I put my arm around her and slowly walked her back to the house, doing my best to console her.

At the office, I gave the order for three guards to be posted at the entrance of the base and instructed Jimmy to contact a local contractor to repair the fence and build a temporary guard shack. Moira interrupted and stated that I had a phone call from an individual who refused to identify himself.

"The caller sounds as though it is urgent, Captain."

"All right, I'll take it...Yes?" I said as I answered the call.

The caller continued, "Ye, you may not know me, but we have spoken before. I'm afraid yer still planning to turn the base over to the British Army. In the meantime, ye had a traitor at yer guardhouse, and we got rid of him. It may get worse. Good-bye."

At this point, I was horrified. All I could think of was to close the base as quickly as possible.

I carried out my responsibilities and called Admiral Schmidt and Admiral Perry and informed them of the recent guardhouse disaster and murder and the threatening phone call. I clearly conveyed my anxiety and the need to accelerate the closing of the base and the transfer of personnel. There was no doubt in my mind that my civilian indigenous employees were a combination of Loyalists or IRA sympathizers. However, it was clear to me that George O'Donnell was currently an IRA member and Willy McGafferty was an IRA member prior to his death.

I called a meeting with all my officers and senior petty officers. I had to remind them that our civilian employees were a mixture of local sympathizers and we needed to be cautious in what we said and did. Again, I reminded them that the base was being returned to the queen and *not* to the British Army. We were going to rapidly dismiss our civilian employees and—I hoped—work with the embassy to procure new employment for them. Also, I wanted to immediately transfer military personnel and their families to Thurso, Scotland, as soon as living accommodations could be secured.

"I must tell all of you that I am disappointed in the progress at the Thurso buildup. I have asked the embassy and Washington to hasten the buildup of operations and living quarters at Thurso. Warrant Officer Emberton and I will be making several trips to Thurso to ensure progress is being made."

Over the next month, things remained hectic, as civilians and military were backing up and preparing to move. Trucks came and went with great frequency, and it was difficult to secure the base. Each department designated certain people to remain until the end to tie up loose ends and provide some security. However, all families would be transferred to Thurso or other duty stations as quickly as possible.

"Admiral Schmidt and his staff in Washington will provide exceptional support in getting orders cut and authorization for families to vacate and move immediately. Although 70 percent of the military is going to Thurso, the remainder is being transferred all around the world."

All seemed to be going well. Buildings were being emptied and vital communications to the fleet continued as best we could.

One late afternoon, Master Chief Charlie Wilson came frantically pushing through my office door. "Captain, Captain, I just came from the gymnasium, where Ian Nelson was swinging from a rafter that runs across the roof of Sampson Hall. Swinging slowly in the morning breeze the open door brought in. A garish bright orange tie, a noose around his neck."

"Chief, are you sure?"

"Yes, sir! The corpsman is there and the XO. Captain, I think you should come with me now."

The hall was a horrifying sight. His face was purple, and the orange tie was symbolic. A crowd had gathered in the meantime. Some were clapping while others were just in shock.

The chief master-of-arms said to me that it looked like murder, not suicide. "Remember, Captain, he was a member of the Orangemen and a fanatic Loyalist."

I ordered Chief Wilson, master-at-arms, to notify the local constabulary and to conduct an investigation.

Chapter 19

Endearment

The religious conflicts continued in Northern Ireland and especially the city of Londonderry. A few weeks after Carter's election, on November 27, 1976, the Irish Republican Army killed two Catholic civilians in separate booby-trap bomb attacks in Lurgan, County Armagh, and in the Bogside area of Derry. The bombs were intended for the security forces. The Peace People held a rally in London that was attended by thirty thousand people. Republican sympathizers held a small counterdemonstration, chanting, "Troops out!"

In the middle of the political problems, the city of Londonderry sensed economic problems ahead if the base closed and embarked on an extensive marketing campaign to influence the US Navy to keep the base in Londonderry. There was good reason to keep the base open. Apart from its contribution to the economy of the city, it had become part of the personality of the city, much more like another suburb than an isolated military base.

I became the key person in the area to be wined and dined and influenced in any way to keep the navy base in Londonderry. The city had some events in the late autumn and invited me and my staff to attend. A local choir put on concerts for us and always sang "God Bless America."

The town of Londonderry and its elected officials took a different point of view and decided to fight for their livelihood by showing how much they loved Americans, how much they needed us. It was important for them to do so for the city's economic welfare, especially with the financially draining troubles going on.

The strategy of the town was to execute a continuous display of acts of endearment to Americans. They wanted to show us how much they respected us, how important we were to Derry, and let us know that no one would ever hurt an American.

In this atmosphere of endearment by the town, hardly a week would go by that my wife and I and my officers would not receive an invitation to some party or official event. And, as if it were planned, the famous hymn "God Bless America" would always be sung at the beginning, at the end, or in the middle of almost any occasion.

Gathering at Guild Hall for U.S. Navy Parade

In the middle of December, there was an elaborate lunch held by the mayor of Londonderry and his key city officials. I and my top officers were special guests. The lunch was at one of those buildings in downtown Londonderry that was built sometime in the Dark Ages.

The lunch featured roasted lamb with all the Irish trimmings of mushrooms, mashed potatoes, and kale with a tasty pudding dessert at the end and plenty of Guinness. At the end of the meal, the waiters filled a shot glass of Jameson for everyone at the table. When all the glasses were filled, the mayor clinked his glass, stood up, and exclaimed, "Let us have a toast."

Everyone stood up and raised his or her glass. "To the United States of America. To the marvelous navy base and its people that we enjoy so much. May it never leave us. Here, here!"

Then, with great gusto, the mayor began to sing "God Bless America," and everyone joined in.

I decided that a toast to the city was the proper thing to follow this with. But before I could get a word out, the mayor cut in.

"Just a minute, Captain," the mayor said. "It's time to sing. Remember, we are a musical city and the home of Phil Coulter. I will sing a song, and then we will go around the table and each of ye will get a chance to have at it."

The mayor then began singing the famous "Derry Air" ("Danny Boy") with a deep, impressive baritone voice. When he finished, everyone applauded long and loud. He then explained that it was the lyrics for "Danny Boy" but the locals called it "Derry Air."

"Next," the mayor looked at me, "Captain, will you give us a little ditty?"

I knew I was going to have to sing from the minute the mayor started this part of lunch. I came up with "East Side, West Side." After my rendition of the song, the singing moved around the U-shaped table and I was pleasantly surprised that my Yankee officers did so well. But things were getting close to Warrant Officer Jimmy Emberton, and I could see Jimmy collapsing under the pressure.

"Do you have a song, Mr. Emberton?" I asked. "It's your turn."

Jimmy turned a bright color of red.

"Yes, sir," he said as he began singing "Jingle Bells" in perhaps the most off-key version anyone had ever heard.

The invitations to concerts, family dinners, and church festivals kept coming. My officers and I were overwhelmed with the hospitality.

However, in the middle of all of this endearment from the city, I still had a downtrodden crew of civilians and military, knowing that the base was going to close.

I thought it was significant that we showed the people of Derry our love and admiration. I called Admiral Perry to explain that I would like to arrange a parade through the city to express our gratitude for over thirty-five years of friendship and *the city we loved so well*. The admiral fully agreed and said he would send the famous Sixth Fleet band to Londonderry when we were ready. I spoke to the mayor, and we set a date for the parade. My officers and crew were extremely excited about this and began to practice marching together on the soccer field. This was highly out of character for a sailor, as our expertise is staggering on ships and not losing our balance. The Sixth Fleet Band arrived, and the mayor arranged to transport the band to the base.

Shawn heard of the celebration and asked me if he could ride Mr. Ed in the parade.

I replied, "Sure, in fact, you can dress up as an Indian and lead the parade."

The whole town of Derry and military people lined the streets. The band played American and Irish songs while tears streamed from their faces. Furthermore, there were no terrorist actions or mishaps on the day of the parade.

The numbers of military personnel, civilians, and family members were diminishing, and I could not ignore the pain in my heart brought about by the deceit of knowing that the base turnover would be secretly carried out between me and the British Army, a devastating command that would injure the pride of both the Americans and the

Irish. In spite of this, I decided to have an official closing ceremony on the base and invite all Londonderry city dignitaries.

Prior to the closing ceremony and the transfer of some of my officers, I hosted a private Christmas party in my quarters and included the mayor and other dignitaries from the town. Mary hired a caterer to provide food under her direction, and Carl Campbell would tend bar. In the middle of the party, there was a loud rap on the door. Mary opened the door, and there stood Chief Master-at-Arms Wilson, holding Father Mullins by the nape of the neck.

"Oh my goodness, what happened to our priest?"

Hearing Mary, I went to the door.

Wilson exclaimed, "I caught Father Mullins stealing the chapel organ and some other religious stuff and putting it in his truck."

I looked at Father Mullins. He was pale and pitiful, with bulging eyes. I immediately hustled the two outside and away from the crowd. "I appreciate your diligence, Chief, but I gave Father permission to take the organ and whatever else he wanted from the chapel."

Wilson immediately released Father Mullins, who hugged me and blessed me with the sign of the cross. I then returned to the festivities filled with holiday cheer and decor. The house was so full of holiday spirit, why not have a Christmas party for all children and invite Santa and his elves? This would be an ideal way to bring Protestant and Catholic children together.

Chapter 20

The Christmas Party

It was the last Christmas before the Londonderry base was scheduled to close down. Mary and Shannon Kelly and a number of other wives held meetings and began plans for the children's party to be held in the gym on the base. Mary contacted the *Derry Journal* and asked them to publicize the Christmas Party so all children from both sides of the religious conflict would be able to enjoy a holiday party on neutral territory.

In this regard, I called Admiral Schmidt to get permission to purchase three hundred navy-blue-and-gold watch caps to be given to the children as a token of the US Navy's love of the people. The admiral approved my request.

On Saturday afternoon, the inside of Sampson Gym was busy with wives and mothers decorating for the party. Tables of food were laid out, and there was a huge pile of gifts by a large Christmas tree, which Jimmy and a few others had found in a city called Limavady not too far out of Londonderry.

In a dressing room off to the side of the gym, Jimmy dressed up as an elf and helped me into a Santa Claus suit he had rented from a costume store in downtown Londonderry. It was a few hours before the children would arrive, but already Jimmy and I were sipping on a bottle of Jameson. I was not all that happy with being the designated Santa Claus.

"George O'Donnell would make a lot better Santa Claus," I said to Jimmy. "Or Carl Campbell. Or even you."

"Santa needs an elf," Jimmy said. "And besides, there is only one appropriate Santa Claus for the base."

Every so often, Mary popped her head inside the dressing room and reminded me to watch myself, as I had a long night in front of me.

It was dark at six o'clock when two school buses left the parking lot of the gym and headed out to pick up the children. The buses were painted navy blue with the insignia of the base on their sides, a three-leaf clover with bolts of lightning across it. Jimmy the Elf drove one of the buses, and George O'Donnell drove the other bus. George was also dressed like an elf. There was a soft rain that fell off and on.

The two buses headed down the hill and over the bridge into the town. A few days before Christmas, everything was quiet in Londonderry, and there had been no incidents for a few days. Colored lights were strung around many of the pubs, and they were reflected in the streets wet with the soft rain. Bells from a number of the churches clanged through the night air, almost like they were announcing some temporary truce of sorts. Somehow, there were no checkpoints set up on the roads that night.

Jimmy stopped in front of one of the large Protestant churches in town, where a group of children were gathered with their parents. The children were quiet as Jimmy came out and helped the parents direct them onto the school bus. They were more than a little scared by the whole thing. They were not used to being put on a bus and driven somewhere, especially with all the problems with the troubles of the city. A number of parents got on the bus with them, and soon, we were heading back to the base.

Half a mile away, George O'Donnell stopped his bus at a Catholic church in the poor Bogside area of Londonderry, not far from the flat of Shannon and Sean Kelly. There was another group of children gathered in front of the church, and George ushered them onto the bus with a number of parents. Like the Protestant children on Jimmy's bus, the Catholic children were quiet and did not seem very eager to get on the bus, not knowing what was in store for them. Their short lives had been so full of bombs and gunfire it was difficult for them to feel something other than this was in store for them, even around Christmas.

The buses arrived around the same time back in the parking lot next to the base gym, and the children slowly got off the buses and went into the gym. Mary and a number of base wives met the children at the entrance to the gym, and each child was given a name tag, a stocking with some toys, and a navy-blue-and-gold wool watch cap. The toys brought some excitement to the children, but many still clung tightly to their parents. No one seemed all that excited to be there. Irish and Catholics just didn't mix in Northern Ireland.

The two groups gathered in separate areas of the gym, quietly standing and watching the other group. Christmas songs blared out of the PA system in the gym, and a disco light hung in the center of the gym, throwing sparkling stars around the room and over the children.

Mary went up to a microphone and welcomed everyone to the party. She pointed out that there was plenty of food on the tables and that a special visitor was arriving.

There was the sound of sleigh bells over the PA system, and then a side door of the gym swung open. The elves, Jimmy and George, came out, followed by me, Santa Claus, carrying a large bag of toys over my back and saying, "Ho, ho, ho!" over and over again. I walked in front of the two groups of children, waving my arm and saying, "Ho, ho, ho!" and then went to a large chair up on stage.

"I hope he hasn't had too much to drink," Mary said to another wife, watching me.

Jimmy walked over to the group of Protestant children and led them in a line to see Santa Claus and tell him what they wanted for Christmas. And Elf George did the same with the Catholic children. The children stood in two lines right next to each other but didn't say anything to each other.

Soon, children were sitting on my lap and telling me what they wanted for Christmas. The wives had found some special gifts for the children, like new soccer balls, dolls, shiny toy cars, and art sets, and the gifts sparked the children as they opened them and began playing with them. The two groups of children were beginning to mingle, laugh, and have a good time.

Carl Campbell was busy at the bar set up in one corner of the gym, pouring Guinness and Jameson. Parents from the two groups were mingling with each other, and there were even toasts given between Catholics and Protestants.

The Christmas carols over the PA system soon gave way to disco music, and there was dancing on the gym floor as the children ran around the gym, playing with their new toys.

Sometime during the party, a large side door swung open and Shawn came in dressed as an elf and riding Mr. Ed, who had some makeshift antlers over his ears so that he looked like an old, gray, over-sized reindeer. Mr. Ed pulled a sleigh filled with more toys and candy, and Mary and the wives tossed them at the children. The children loved the big reindeer and followed Shawn and Mr. Ed as they went around the gym.

There were still a few children who had not gotten to talk to Santa. Shannon Kelly pushed her five-year-old son, Conor Kelly, toward me. When Conor was sitting on my lap, I asked him what he wanted for Christmas.

"I wish my sister could be here tonight," Conor said.

"Where is your sister?" I asked.

"She's home," said Conor.

I gave Conor a gift and another one for his sister.

"You give this to your sister," I told Conor.

Shannon Kelly smiled as she got her son from Santa's lap.

"That's nice of you to think of Megan," Shannon said.

"Why can't Megan be here?" I asked.

"She's at home in her wheelchair," said Shannon. "The cold night air is not good for her."

I made a note of what Shannon had just said and motioned George over.

"Find out where Shannon Kelly lives," I told him. "But don't ask her. Find out from someone else."

"No problem," said George. "I know exactly where she lives. Not far from me in fact."

The party continued on after all the children had sat on my lap, gotten their present, and told me what they wanted for Christmas. Shawn and Mr. Ed were one of the great hits of the party, and Shawn ended up giving rides on Mr. Ed around the gym. The two groups that were so separate at the beginning of the party were now mixed in one big mass, and it was impossible to tell Catholic children from Protestant children and impossible to really be concerned about the two groups.

⌒⋀⋌⋋

Two hours after the planned end of the party, the children and parents began to file out of the gym and back into the buses.

I went over to Mary.

"Have any more of those hobbit dolls that Tara told us to buy?"

Mary went away and came back with a red package with a large green ribbon on it.

"Last one," she said.

I took the package and got on board George's bus as the children cheered.

"Really, Captain," George said. "I think it might be time to drive the old sleigh into the garage."

I did not say anything but simply helped the children onto the bus. Shannon Kelly got on the bus with Conor and was surprised to see her boss.

Soon, we were off back down the hill and over the bridge across the River Foyle and through Londonderry. The soft rain was still falling, and the streets were black mirrors reflecting the colored lights strung on the buildings and pubs along the streets. Bells from churches were still clanging, and British troops were nowhere to be seen.

The bus stopped at the Catholic Church in the Bogside area of Londonderry. The children filed off. They were laughing, screaming, and talking about their toys and the giant gray reindeer they saw that night. If one didn't know it, one would swear that there was a completely different group of children on the bus going back than the group on this bus a few hours earlier.

The parents thanked me as I stood in the soft rain, saying goodbye and "Merry Christmas" to them.

"God bless you, Captain," many parents said to me.

As Shannon and Conor began to get off the bus, I stopped them and asked them to remain on the bus.

Shannon was perplexed.

"What's this all about, Captain?" she asked.

"You'll see," I said.

When the bus door closed and George started up the engine, I told him, "We're taking Shannon and Conor home."

George was somewhat startled by this.

"Not sure if that is a good idea, Captain," he said. "There are safer areas in town."

"Drive," I said to George.

In a few minutes, the big navy bus was stopped on a narrow cobbled street in the Bogside area of Londonderry.

"Turn the engine off, George," I said. "Santa has one more child to see tonight."

Shannon seemed nervous.

"I'm not sure that it's a real good idea, Captain," she said.

There was no telling what state her husband, Sean, was in that night, and who knew if any of his IRA associates were at the house and whether they were sober. She looked at George for guidance, and George simply winked and nodded his head that it was OK for the captain to go up and see Megan.

The four of us went through the little black door and up the narrow steps to the flat on the second floor. Shannon asked us to wait in the hall for a minute while she went in and got Megan ready to see Santa Claus.

Sean Kelly was sitting in the kitchen in a dirty white T-shirt and watching a soccer game on their little black-and-white television set. There were a few empty bottles of Guinness on the table.

Conor ran for his father.

"Santa is outside," he said. "He's come to see Megan!"

After he said this, he ran into the other room to get his sister.

"Captain McKeown and George O'Donnell are outside," Shannon said.

"What?" said Sean.

"I couldn't stop him," she said. "The captain is Santa Claus this year. He asked Conor what he wished for for Christmas, and Conor said he wished that Megan was at the event tonight."

"So he came to visit Megan?" Sean said.

"He's outside the door," said Shannon.

As she said this, the door to Megan's room opened, and Conor came out, pushing his sister in her wheelchair. There was a startled look on Megan's face. She was not sure what was happening.

Shannon smiled at Megan and kissed her.

"Are you ready to meet Santa Claus?" she asked.

With this, she opened the door and Santa's elf and I walked into the little kitchen of the flat. George winked at Sean, realizing that all of this was hard to believe.

"Santa," Shannon said, "this is my husband, Sean Kelly."

"Glad to meet you, Mr. Kelly," I said.

"You too, Santa," Sean replied.

"And this must be Megan," I said, looking at Megan.

The little girl slowly shook her head. She could not believe that Santa had come to pay a special visit to her.

I pulled up a chair and sat down next to Megan.

"I missed you at the party tonight and wanted to make sure that I visited you," I said.

The little girl slowly shook her head.

"Thank you, Santa," she said. "That's nice of you."

"I need to know if you have been a good girl," I said to Megan.

"I think so," said Megan.

"Good," I said. "And what do you want for Christmas?"

The little girl looked at her mother.

"I want something magic," she said.

"Ah," I said. "Something magic indeed."

I gave the big red package to Megan. She opened the package and pulled out the large hobbit doll.

"A hobbit!" she excitedly exclaimed.

"Something magic," Shannon Kelly said and smiled, pulling a small camera from a cupboard. "We have to get a picture of this."

"Wait," I said. "Put your navy watch cap on first. This cap will keep you warm in the winter."

The little girl put her arms around my neck, and Shannon snapped a picture.

"Thank you, Santa," she said. "Thank you very much."

"I think Santa needs to get back to the North Pole," Shannon said. "And little girls need to go to bed."

Conor wheeled his sister back into her room.

"Glad to meet you, Captain McKeown," said Sean. "I've heard a lot about you from Shannon."

"Shannon is a great employee," I said.

"You gave Megan a magic Christmas," Sean said.

"What's wrong with Megan?" I asked.

"The troubles," Sean said. "Megan was struck by a bullet from a Protestant protestor a few years ago. I saw the whole thing. She'll never walk again."

I just shook my head. We needed more magic in all of Northern Ireland.

Chapter 21

Approaching Storm

However, magic was tough to come by in Northern Ireland after the Christmas season. On January 1 of the New Year, a fifteen-month-old baby boy was killed in a car bomb explosion at Harmin Park, Glengormley, near Belfast. The car bomb had been planted by the Irish Republican Army and an inadequate warning given. Also, a terrible, depressing event occurred when a bomb went off in Derry's famous Guild Hall. On February 2, Jeffrey Agate, the managing director of the American DuPont factory in Derry was shot dead by members of the Irish Republican Army outside his home in the Talbot Park area of Derry. The killing marked the beginning of a series of attacks on businessmen in Derry with further killings on March 2 and March 14. On February 3, Joseph Morrissey, a Catholic civilian, was found stabbed and with his throat cut on the Glencairn Road in Belfast. Members of the Ulster Volunteer Force gang, known as the "Shankill Butchers," were responsible for the killing. On April 8, 1977, two Royal Ulster Constabulary officers were shot dead by the Irish Republican Army near Moneymore and County Derry.

But despite the surrounding violence, the feelings between Catholics and Protestants generated by the Christmas party did not recede into a fading memory but continued to ferment into a new collective feeling. George O'Donnell had never seen anything like it in all his years on the base. It was heart warming to see so many children with blue and gold watch caps.

I sensed a new spirit come over the base. I saw it everywhere—in the EM club, the athletic fields, and the social functions. Mary was caught up in the new spirit like most other mothers on the base. Seeing the two groups of children together and visiting Megan Kelly, had given Mary a new feeling about the base. No longer did it seem some temporary stop. Rather it was beginning to feel like that home she had longed for all these years.

I began to think that it was a logical and natural thing for the base to stay open rather than close down. After all, the real danger was not in keeping the base open but really in closing it and turning it over to the British Army. The IRA had made themselves more than clear on this matter.

I did not tell anyone about my change of attitude, not even Mary and not even my good friend Jimmy. I continued to proceed ahead as planned to turn the base over to the British Army. I felt more than ever the lie I was perpetuating and the effect of this lie on hundreds of people. It was wearing at me. I knew something had to be done, but I wasn't sure what it was.

The work in Thurso, Scotland, was not only over cost but also behind schedule by a few months, and there was little choice but to continue operations in Londonderry. There were a number of phone calls with Lieutenant Roberts at Thurso. He continued to have trouble with regulations and contractors, and materials were slow in being delivered as costs continued to escalate. It was obvious that I would have to send Jimmy Emberton to Thurso sooner than planned in order to correct any financial problems. In view of the potential increase in terrorism and the need to close the base as soon as possible, I refused to dig into any financial manipulations at Thurso or the Embassy.

⌒⌒⌒

For Easter of 1977, the wives organized an Easter-egg hunt on the base. Jimmy got the idea to have Mary and me dress up in Easter bunny suits with Mary in the blue suit and me in the pink suit. My first response was to offer up Jimmy to walk the plank. But the Derry wives were adamant that I dress up as the pink Easter bunny. With Mary leading the charge, they were an impossible group to deal with.

On Easter morning, I was squirming into a large pink Easter bunny suit that Jimmy had rented from this costume store in Derry. There was a considerable number of cuss words coming out of my mouth as Jimmy helped me make the transformation from commanding officer to commanding bunny. This transformation only made Jimmy laugh all the harder at the large, floppy-eared pink Easter bunny.

Soon, Mr. and Mrs. Easter Bunny were walking around the grounds outside the gym, dispensing Easter eggs and little gifts from their baskets. The base children were screaming loudly. They loved the event and even more so to see two giant Easter bunnies. But the laughter from my sailors at seeing their skipper in the pink suit was even greater than the excited screams of the children.

Half an hour later, on the gym floor in a stupid-looking oversized chair, the big pink Easter bunny was receiving children on his lap. Many needed to be pushed toward the big bunny by anxious parents or timid grandparents.

⌒⁊⋀⋋⌒

It was early morning in April a few weeks after Easter, and Londonderry was smothered under a thick fog that hung over the town like a wet gray blanket. I had my shorts and hiking shoes on. The sun was just coming up in the east, and the famous Irish green had a golden, burnished color to it, like the beginning of weathered green copper. It was early in the morning, and my family and base were still asleep with only the gate guard on duty.

On top of the hill, you could almost see the entire base rimmed inside the chain-link fence—the collection of the brick housing quarters, the gym where so many social events had taken place since I arrived, the officer's club where George O'Donnell presided over the bar with the authority of a ship captain, and the athletic fields where so many sporting events had taken place and where the base soccer team practiced and took themselves from a hopeless bunch of laughable Yanks to the top soccer team for all the service bases in the United Kingdom. In the distance was the antenna array in the field where Shawn kept his old gray horse, Mr. Ed, and near the field was the squat, plain brick building housing the communications center, where red lights might be flashing at any time. Off in the distance was the old walled town of Derry on the west bank of the River Foyle, which meandered through the landscape like a sparkling silver snake in the early morning sun.

I sat on the top of the hill for a while, watching the colors of the city and base change with the rising sun of a new day. Thoughts came and went like they were flashes from a display of northern lights, illuminating some things hidden for many years briefly enough for me to sense their existence but not long enough for me to investigate the details of their architecture. Then I walked down the hill and back through the gate and onto the base.

～⁊⟨⟩～

An hour later, I arrived at my office. It was still early in the morning, and my staff had not arrived. I went into my office and closed the door. I sat at my desk, looking out the window at the morning sun spreading its light over the athletic grounds and beyond them the array of antennae in the field. It was not like me to ponder things like this, as decisions usually came quickly for me. But this was different somehow, and my thoughts went back almost ten years.

The office window seemed like the porthole of a ship. As a young officer, I had disagreed with my immediate superior then, and now I seemed to be going to Washington, DC, to disagree with another of my superiors.

In many ways, the Londonderry base was like a ship heading into a great storm. I was now the captain of this particular ship, but I was still being commanded by my superiors in Washington, DC.

The weather during the months I had been on the base had been mild and calm with the Irish rains falling gently over Derry and the base in the winter, but now the brilliant blue Irish sky of spring capped the supernatural emerald green of the landscape. But even with the beautiful weather, I sensed my current ship was heading toward a violent storm. The thunder of the storm could be heard almost every day and late into the nights with explosions in nearby Londonderry marking the troubles. And the lightning of the approaching storm seemed to be the magnificent flashes of the northern lights across the sky in the evenings.

In all of this, Catholics and Protestants continued to die in the violence, many of them children and innocent civilians. The threatening calls continued to come that the base would be blown to bits if I carried out my true mission and turned it over to the British Army. But what if it was simply kept open?

I also knew there was a silent storm heading toward the city with the serious losses the base closing would cause to the town of Londonderry, which had such a long relationship with the navy. It was a strange relationship, I thought, this island of Yanks in the middle of the battling Catholics and Protestants of Northern Ireland.

Phil Coulter's song "The City I Loved So Well" applied to Americans as much as anyone else. But it had worked so beautifully for so many years. All these American sailors coming so far away from one home and finding another home. So many of them had married Irish women and now had families and relatives and were entangled with the town and Ireland as much as the old Irish myths were entangled with Derry, in a similar way that America too was so entangled with Ireland, whether she knew it or not.

⌒〞⌒

I saw this entanglement each day on the base and everywhere I went. It was as if the Americans had planted a tree when they first came to Derry and now this tree had grown into a great specimen with many branches and gnarly roots that scattered all over the landscape. I saw connections to the roots of this great tree at the social functions in the base gym with all the red-haired Irish wives showing their American husbands special Irish dances. I saw the connections in the little apartments in Londonderry where many of my sailors' families lived off the base. I saw these roots in the camaraderie at the pubs in Derry between the Yanks and the Irish. The Irish saw so much of what they longed to become in the Yanks. And the Yanks saw so much of what they once were in the Irish.

The great approaching storm that moved toward my new ship was both similar and different from the one that moved toward my first ship.

Two American presidents and all of my commanding officers had ordered me to get away from the storm of the troubles in Northern Ireland by escaping to the new base in Scotland. But I somehow knew that the base would always be safe even in the middle of all the bombings and that the relationships between the Irish and Americans must be allowed to continue to grow like they had grown for so many years.

Violence would come not from keeping the base open but from closing it and turning it over to the British Army. Yes, there was a strange but real love of the Irish for the American Yanks who had been a part of their town for over thirty-five years. I knew this; I could feel it in my Irish-Catholic blood. I felt that violence was ahead if I carried out my secret orders of turning the base over to the British Army rather than the queen, because of the many threats I had received. This was the real storm I knew was approaching.

I picked up the white telephone on my desk, and in a few minutes, the admiral's voice came on.

"Tom, good to hear your voice," said the gravelly voice of the admiral. "We've been following things in Northern Ireland. Things aren't getting any better. It's good we're getting out soon."

"I need to talk to you, Admiral," I said.

"Talk," said the admiral.

"It's something too important to discuss over the phone," I said.

"You know our phone lines are secure," the admiral said.

"Yes, I know, but it's something I need to meet with you about in person."

"I don't want you away from the base with everything happening."

"I can fly to Washington for just a day or so. It's very important I see you."

There was a moment of silence on the phone.

"This Friday," the admiral said. "Fifteen hundred hours."

"I'll be there."

When the call ended, I pushed the buzzer on my phone and told Shannon to make travel arrangements for my trip to Washington, DC.

That evening, I sat out in my backyard with Mary, watching the great rippling green sheets of the northern lights.

"I've gotta go to DC for a few days," I said. "Talk to Admiral Schmidt."

"Base closing stuff?" Mary asked.

"Yeah, just some housekeeping stuff."

"I'm getting to like it here," Mary said.

"Yeah, I am too, but I think it is getting more dangerous by the day. You and the kids may have to go to Thurso a month or so before I close the base."

Mary replied, "Here we go again, always separated, always moving. Will you ever retire so we can live a normal life as a family?"

Chapter 22

The Washington Trip

A few days later, I watched Ireland sink into the Atlantic Ocean from the window of the navy plane I was on, heading to Washington, DC, for my meeting with Admiral Schmidt at the Pentagon.

Events and people on the base and from the city of Derry had changed my mind that the base needed to be closed down. I remembered the mingling of the Catholic and Protestant children at the Christmas party and dressing up as a fairy for Halloween and the Easter bunny for Easter. I remembered the funny songs everyone sang at the mayor's meeting and the base soccer team and all of the celebrations they had. I thought of the fun family trips into the surrounding countryside of Ireland, to include the famous Causeway coastline, and the antics of Shawn's gray horse, Mr. Ed.

Yes, there was danger living in Northern Ireland, but I had become convinced that the people of Derry had a true affection for the Yanks and that the base played a key role in the local economy. I knew that many would lose their jobs if the base closed down. It was a different feeling than the one I had arrived with nine months before, and these feelings were in conflict with the direct orders I had to close the base down.

Yes, I turned over the USS *Leary* to Spain and the base in Vietnam to the South Vietnamese navy.

These actions were turnovers, not the actions of a hatchet man in closing down a functional base. But now, for the first time in my life, I was faced with a base I did not want to close down. I felt I had to make an attempt to keep this base open. I was on my way to a meeting with Admiral Schmidt in Washington, DC, to plead my case for keeping the base open. The course somehow had to be changed.

I arrived at Admiral Schmidt's office a few minutes before fifteen hundred hours as ordered. Seated in the office were the same gentlemen who concurred with the admiral and provided guidance to me over one year ago: Robert Hunt from the Office of the Secretary of the State Department, Ralph Douglas from the CIA, Peter Spencer from the Office of the Secretary of Defense (SECDEF), and Ian Radcliff from the British embassy. They all greeted me as I entered the room, and Admiral Schmidt shook my hand.

"Tom, we are happy to see you and are anxious to hear what's on your mind."

"Gentlemen, there is no doubt about the effectiveness and the operational need for a naval communication station to support our naval missions in the North Atlantic and Baltic areas. This is particularly important for our submarines, which rely heavily on our VLF communications capabilities. Thurso is very slow in picking up Derry's operational load. I have made a few visits to Thurso and plan to do more when I return. However, I am here to recommend maintaining our base in Londonderry. Of course, this is contrary to my original orders. The people of Londonderry go out of their way to make sure our American sailors are not harmed. We have had several lunches and dinners with the city dignitaries, and we have children's events and athletic competitions on the base. We are a neutral territory for both the Provisional IRA and the Loyalists. Yes, we have had some minor incidents on the base, but these were strictly related to the religious factions. Gentlemen, we are at the decision point today. Do you want me to continue on with closing Derry expediently, or shall we continue our critical naval operations?"

As I looked around the table, I could see eyebrows twitching, and Admiral Schmidt's mouth dropped open. "Tom, are you serious?" the admiral exclaimed.

Ian Radcliff spoke up. "Admiral, we do need to move royal army units closer to the city of Derry."

Then Peter Spencer explained that we could not afford to lose vital communications support from Derry or Thurso. "Keeping Derry open is not a bad idea," he said.

Robert Hunt reminded all of us that it was the president himself who wanted Derry closed. He did not want an international crisis between our country and the British.

Admiral Schmidt stood up and asked me a defining question. "Tom, do you see any end to the troubles?"

Before I could answer, Ralph Douglas, from the CIA, stood up and said, "From the CIA point of view, the troubles are getting worse."

I then responded to the admiral's question. "No, sir, I do not see any end to this desperate struggle."

The admiral responded, "Tom, carry out your orders. You are doing a good job; we are proud of you. Get Thurso in gear, and expedite the closing of Derry. Move the people off the base as quickly as possible, and you know my staff will support you 100 percent."

We all shook hands, and I left the office.

My flight back to Ireland left the next day, and I had the afternoon free. I decided to drive out to see our home in Springfield, Virginia, and stop by the Little League baseball field to see if there was a game going on.

The home was rented, and I was satisfied with its appearance; a woman was working in the flower bed. She looked surprisingly like Mary. I thought of stopping to say hello but decided not to and drove to the baseball field a few blocks away.

I stopped my car, got out, and watched the game through the chain-link fence. The Springfield Dragons were playing the Fairfax Tigers and kicking the heck out of them. One of the fathers I knew was coaching, and I recognized a number of Shawn's friends on the team.

When the game was over, I thought of going over and saying hello to a few of the boys, but it seemed enough to just watch the game and go back to my hotel.

Maybe the family would be back here soon. Shawn would be back on the baseball team, and Mary would be busy with carpools and PTA meetings again. And maybe I wanted all of this to happen in some way. Maybe Mary wanted it to happen. It was difficult to know what

I wanted, what she wanted, especially since the base and Londonderry had become such a dangerous place.

Chapter 23

Parcel Creates Expediency

Back on the base in Londonderry, there was speculation about my trip to Washington.

"Just some administrative stuff," I told everyone.

No one knew the real purpose of my trip except Jimmy Emberton.

I immediately called a meeting with Shannon Kelly, Tom Johnson, and Jimmy to go over the value of the expenditures compared to the operational progress at Thurso. I asked Shannon to work overtime as necessary. She needed the overtime work with her husband out of a job and all the medical expenses for Megan. The first night she started working overtime, she worked late at the office to get the weekly expense report ready for me.

Shannon left the office around ten and walked toward her car in the parking lot. Maybe a hundred yards away, she saw a figure walking across the base carrying something toward the gym. She ducked behind her car so she would not be seen. The figure stopped next to the gym building and put something down next to it. Then the figure walked down the road toward the parking lot. As he passed, Shannon recognized him as one of the Orangemen who used to be a good chap with Ian Nelson. It was a dark night, but his shiny bald head was unmistakable. He walked past her car and then disappeared into the darkness.

⌒⫯⫯⏢

Shannon drove straight to her flat in the Bogside, ran up the stairs, and began to tell her husband what she had just witnessed. He listened to her story and advised Shannon that I needed to be notified immediately. Sean went straight to the phone.

The phone by my bedside rang.

I answered, "Hello, this is the captain."

"I hate to bother you at this hour, Captain," Sean said, "but Shannon was leaving the office tonight and saw one of the Orangemen place a parcel beside Sampson Hall and then sneak out the back to the parking lot. She believes the man was an old chap of the late Ian Nelson."

I thanked Sean for the information and immediately placed a call to the British Army. I asked for the commanding general. "General Rutledge, I have an emergency on the base. I believe a bomb has been placed near Sampson Hall, and I need the help of your detonation team at once."

The general replied, "Aye, aye, sir."

I thought his reply was odd, but I knew he wasn't joking, just trying to be friendly with his "Aye, aye."

The detonation team arrived in less than twenty minutes. They were dressed in their protective gear and moved the parcel to the center of the soccer field. The team then cleared the field of all personnel and ignited the contents of the parcel. A huge explosion followed. Several glass windows on the base and in the city were shattered because of the blast. I decided to call the *Derry Press* and the local garda to explain the circumstances and assure them that no one was injured or killed. I then placed a call to Admiral Schmidt and explained the incident. I assured him that the situation was under control. "I guess this was my welcome back present from Washington."

"Tom, this is no joke! There is nothing to discuss after this incident," he said. "The damn base needs to be shut down immediately. Things need to be accelerated."

I was still in shock after the explosion. Everything had seemed to be moving along so well in the past few months.

"Get most of your people off the base," the admiral continued. "Operate with a skeleton crew until the handover."

"Yes, sir," was the only response I had for the admiral. The economics of the base, the community spirit, the long connection of the base to Londonderry—all of this paled next to the explosion and the admiral's remarks.

Chapter 24

Disestablishment Ceremony

The death of Ian Nelson was ruled a suicide by the police, but the Orangemen and other Protestant groups knew it was murder and the work of the IRA. It all led to another round of shootings and bombings in Londonderry.

Even the queen was not safe. On August 9, she began a two-day visit to Northern Ireland. It was the first visit by the queen in eleven years. The Irish Republican Army planted a small bomb in a garden on the campus of the new Ulster University, which the queen visited as part of her jubilee celebrations. It exploded after she left. Although the bomb caused no injuries, members of the Social Democratic and Labor Parties refused to attend a reception in her honor.

I began cutting personnel from the base, making every effort I could to find jobs for them. With Ian Nelson gone, I promoted Shannon Kelly to head of base operations. She knew the expenses of running the base better than anyone else.

I worked closely with my executive officer, Bob McManus, to salvage items on the base under the directions of US Navy logistics. The transmitter towers had a lot of copper in them, and he was able to sell it for a good price and make the navy some money. Since Lieutenant McManus was the XO, he knew exactly what was left at the base, and as navy directives required, he prepared a complete inventory of all existing buildings, equipment, and surplus material, such as furniture and perishable items.

I called Lieutenant Roberts at Thurso a number of times to check on the progress of getting the base up and operational. However, he had already received a call from Admiral Schmidt, who was requiring faster progress. Roberts was now working around the clock to prepare Thurso for increased operational duties.

After the bomb incident, civilians were leaving the base in droves. Each time someone departed, there would be a party at night in the tearoom located in the middle of the housing area. I often stopped by and joined everyone in singing. There were few dry eyes at these parties.

There was a big parade in downtown Londonderry to commemorate the closing of the base. The participants included the local police band, the British Army troops, all the base sailors, and local church organizations. Shawn rode his notorious gray horse, Mr. Ed, in the parade. And the Sixth Fleet Band came up from the Mediterranean. Admiral Schmidt flew over and observed the parade, standing between me and the mayor of Derry.

I gave a speech and quoted the last verse of a popular song at the time called "The Town I Loved So Well" by Irish singer Phil Coulter.

Its words captured the way I and many of my personnel felt at the time.

> Now the music's gone, but they carry on
> For their spirit's been bruised, never broken.
> They will not forget, but their hearts are set
> On tomorrow and peace once again
> For what's done is done and what's won is won
> And what's lost is lost and gone forever.
> I can only pray for a bright, brand-new day
> In the town I love so well.

The parade served as a type of formal closing of the base, and after the parade, there was a mass departure of the remaining civilian employees. As Admiral Schmidt had ordered, I moved the base toward operating with a skeleton crew of essential sailors to keep the communications operations going and little more than this.

⌐⫯⊹

The toughest thing for me was saying good-bye to Mary and my family and putting them on the Stranraer ferry in Belfast headed for Thurso.

Mary was saddened to leave the group of navy wives and mothers she had become good friends with but was relieved to hear that some of them would be going to Thurso. More than anything, though, she wanted to return to our home in Springfield. She wanted me to coach

Little League baseball again. She wanted me to build that deck off the back of the house I had planned earlier. She wanted to go home.

The marriage had gone through a number of ups and downs in Londonderry and seemed stuck together with tape and glue and a lingering hope that someday we would have a real home and a real marriage. But the hope came and went like those northern lights. Sometimes, it was powerful and made things bearable, but other times, it seemed gone altogether.

It was a cloudy day in Belfast at the dock when I put them on the ferry for Thurso, another one of those familiar farewell moments for the family. We all knew them well. There had been so many of them throughout my career.

I told them I would be coming in a few weeks, as soon as I closed the base. Shawn asked if Mr. Ed could go to Thurso, and I told Shawn I would check into it. Colleen was excited that a number of her friends were going to Thurso. Tara held her hobbit in one arm and put her other arm around her daddy's neck.

I kissed Mary and held her for a while.

"This is the last stop, the last time," I said to her. "I promise."

Mary gave me a weak, forced smile. She had heard this so many times before.

"I mean it," I said.

But this didn't do much to convince her.

When the ferry pulled away from the dock and was off across the North Sea, I thought to myself how much I also wanted to go home. But I knew I could not take a life behind a desk back at the

Pentagon, pushing papers like Captain Barker. There had to be some other alternative.

Chapter 25

Expanding Thurso

A s the pressure grew stronger to close the base at Derry, I needed to expedite the build out at Thurso, including housing, base support facilities, and telecommunications. My fundamental orders remained the same: to close the base at Derry, simultaneously expand the base at Thurso, and eventually take command of the latter. After my Washington sojourn failed to successfully plead a case for keeping Londonderry open and with a recent increase in local conflicts, I arranged to take regular trips across the Irish Sea. Admiral Perry was quite willing to provide helicopter lifts every week. I decided to form a team with Lieutenant Tom Johnson looking after telecommunications and CWO Jimmy Emberton monitoring logistics. Both joined with Thurso officers to ensure rapid progress and prudent expenditure of funds. Admiral Schmidt required daily situation reports.

Prior to our team leaving one morning, Admiral Schmidt called and said he was thinking of giving me a woman executive officer when I took command at Thurso.

"What do you think, Tom? She would be the first woman to be an executive officer of a naval communications station."

"I don't have any objection, Admiral, but I'd like to meet her first. We have women officers now, but executive officer is a very demanding job. She needs to take over my job when I'm absent, but mostly she needs to be a strong disciplinarian."

"I know," said the admiral. "I want you to get in touch with her. She's on the staff in London, and you guys can arrange to meet. Keep me informed."

"Yes, sir. I'll call her."

Jimmy, Tom, and I met the helicopter at Aldergrove Airport and took off for Scotland. The trip from Belfast, Northern Ireland, to Thurso, Scotland, was one of the most beautiful trips I had ever taken, and I had taken a lot of trips in my years as a naval officer. After lifting off from Belfast in our Fairchild helicopter, we flew low over the Irish Sea. The day was crystal clear, and the brilliant green coast of northeast Ireland against the blue of the Irish Sea was one of the most spectacular sights I had ever seen.

We flew over the Firth of Clyde with the coast of Scotland off to the right and the Isle of Arran to our left. Soon, we were over Scotland with the beautiful Loch Lomond and the Trossachs National Park below us. In twenty minutes, we were over the town of Inverness, heading for the northern part of Scotland. Half an hour later, I could see the city of Thurso on the coast of the North Sea. It was sparkling in the morning sunlight. It was a long and tiring but picturesque, trip. We landed on the antenna field in Thurso and were met by Erick Roberts, the XO in Thurso. I instructed him to talk to the pilots and arrange to have the helicopter fueled for the return trip. I also asked if the officer's club was open, so we could meet, get a current update, and get a cocktail. The weather in Thurso was extremely windy and cold, apparently the norm. During our meeting at the club, I explained to Erick that I would schedule the change of command sometime the next month.

"Admiral Schmidt is extremely pleased with your performance, and he has assured me that your next set of orders will be favorable. The admiral also informed me that I may have a female as my XO. She is currently on the staff in London. I plan to meet her in Edinburgh for an interview in the latter part of this week. In the meantime, I will need a navy car to tour the facilities and my new home. Lieutenant Tom Johnson will be looking after telecommunications, and CWO Jimmy Emberton will be monitoring logistics. Now, if you will excuse me, gentlemen, I would like to go see my wife and family in our new quarters."

I arrived at the new quarters to be greeted by Mary, dressed like an Eskimo, and the children in much the same garb. I gave her a kiss along with each of the kids. Mary only commented on how cold it was in Thurso and that the house did not have a fireplace. I told Mary that I would see to it that we had a fireplace installed as soon as possible. I asked Mary if she was able to find a jacket for Tara's hobbit. She smiled and said, "It's so good to have you home. We all miss you terribly when you are away."

In the latter part of the week, I called Lieutenant Commander Barbara Gregory to arrange an interview in Edinburgh, which was about halfway between London and Thurso.

I then called CWO Jimmy Emberton and told him we were leaving the following day by car for Edinburgh.

Jimmy replied, "Yes, sir, I am ready when you are. Should I bring my clubs?"

"Of course and bring mine as well.

After an eight-hour drive, we arrived in Edinburgh, and I met with Lieutenant Commander Gregory, a very attractive woman neatly dressed in her female officer blues. Her hair had a touch of gray and her blue eyes softened her very business like expression. I was impressed with her resumé and her eagerness to take on this position of authority. Following the interview, Jimmy, Barbara, and I had dinner and discussed the Londonderry and Thurso challenges and the associated dangers of closing Derry. At the conclusion of dinner, I explained to Barbara that I needed her to report to Thurso as soon as possible and be my senior officer. "I will discuss my decision with Admiral Schmidt, and you should be receiving orders in the very near future."

The next morning, Jimmy and I took the east-coast route from Edinburgh back to Thurso. During our trip, we happened to pass St. Andrews. Jimmy turned to me and said, "Captain, I have our clubs in the trunk."

"You know, you have a good idea, Jimmy. Let's stop and see if we can get a starting time."

We parked the car and walked up to the starter's shack.

"Is this where we pay our green fees?" Jimmy asked.

A Scottish fellow with a white beard and dancing blue eyes looked quizzically at us and asked, "Were you on last night's lottery?"

Jimmy replied, "We're not interested in gambling; we just want to play golf."

The Scottish gentleman then inquired if we were Americans. Jimmy emphatically emphasized that we were American navy and needed some R and R. The old gentleman pondered our request and then turned to us. "OK, give me twenty-eight pounds and git on the first tee before anyone notices I have broken every rule in the book."

As we were about to tee off, the old gentleman shouted back, "By the way, I served in the Royal Navy meself."

It was a thrill of a lifetime to play this magnificent and historic course. After finishing the eighteenth hole, I said to Jimmy, "Wouldn't it be wonderful to get a tour of the royal and ancient clubhouse?"

Jimmy said, "No problem, Captain. Let's give it a go."

"Let's not press our luck, Jimmy."

We walked up to the main door, and Jimmy banged the door knocker three times. This stiffly attired gentleman in a white, high-colored uniform opened the door indignantly. "Can I help you?"

Jimmy answered, "This here is my captain, and we'd like to get a tour of your place."

The gentleman replied, "That's impossible, unless the secretary himself approves it."

Jimmy told the gentleman to get the secretary. As the gentleman was about to slam the door in our faces, the secretary magically appeared.

I said, "Excuse me, sir. I am Captain Tom McKeown of the US Navy base at Thurso."

Jimmy politely piped in with a second request for a tour. The stiffly dressed doorman apologized to the secretary for the unexpected interruption. At that moment, the secretary turned to me. "It will be a pleasure, Captain; come on in."

However, prior to stepping over the threshold, the stern doorman told Jimmy to take his dirty damn golf shoes off before entering. At the conclusion of our personal tour, the secretary invited Jimmy and me to share in a round of a special R and A Scotch.

≈

The next morning, I called Admiral Schmidt and requested he process a change of station orders for Lieutenant Commander Gray as soon as possible.

The admiral said he would take care of it and asked, "Where are you now, Tom?"

"I'm in Thurso."

The admiral ordered me to return to Derry immediately, as the situation was getting worse. I returned home to say good-bye to Mary and the kids. As my headlights turned the corner, I could see Mary in the rearview mirror, standing in the doorway, just shaking her head, with her hands on her hips.

Chapter 26

The Plot Thickens

With all military dependents, mostly women, children, and elderly safely off the base—either transferred to Thurso, Scotland, or on to another navy assignment, the base population declined to a mix of thirty white hats, two young lieutenants, and guards to watch critical areas of communications equipment and security material and maintain access control at the gate. Although the base was practically empty and vacant, it was still my responsibility to protect the property until the UK government decided on its disposition.

The base and all its facilities were especially vulnerable at this time. The IRA had made their intentions perfectly clear. I assigned the remaining crew to specific areas: patrols of the perimeter fencing, the communications center, the main gate, and the barracks. The two officers carried forty-five-caliber sidearms, and the patrolling teams had M16s.

I set up a small office at the receiver site in Roscommon. The office included a couple of cots, where Jimmy and I stayed with our suitcases, and a jeep. We were ready to roll as soon as the powers to be gave us instructions. I had worked out an assignment for Jimmy at a base in Tennessee so that he could return home when the base was closed down. Jimmy told me he would rather go to Thurso with me, and reminded me that his wife, Lisa, was from Scotland.

I offered to take George to Thurso with me, but he declined the offer.

"My home is here," George said. "And besides, there is much unfinished business to attend to."

I offered to take Shannon Kelly and her family to Thurso with me and make her head of operations on the new base. But like George, she declined as well. However, through a number of phone calls to the mayor, I was able to get Shannon an interview and eventually a position as an auditor with the city of Londonderry.

The secret about the British Army taking over the base was maintained through all of this. No one ever thought the British Army would take over the base; they thought it was probably going back to the city, and the city would be able to use it for housing, warehouses, and fields for public events, parks, and agriculture.

But the IRA was not fooled and knew the secret plan was always to turn the base over to the Brits. One night, a meeting of key Londonderry IRA leaders took place in the back room of a pub in the Bogside area of Londonderry.

George O'Donnell smiled and shook his head as he raised his pint of Guinness.

"Here's a toast to the late son of a bitch Orangeman Ian Nelson," he said. "He knew better than anyone that a bomb ensured the base would be closed down and turned over to the Protestant Brits."

"A real stronghold for them in Derry," said Sean Kelly.

"What's to do?" asked someone in the room.

"Nothing's gonna stop the Brit tanks from rolling onto the base," said George. "But when they roll onto the base, they might just roll over the rubble of bombed buildings."

"I'll get the boys together," Sean Kelly said.

"Be ready to go soon," George said. "Things are moving fast."

After the meeting, George and Sean walked back to their flats. Both lived a few blocks from the pub. It was a warm evening, and children were still outside playing in the narrow cobblestone street.

"I have mixed emotions about this whole thing," George said. "Captain McKeown is a good man, a good friend. The base reflects his leadership."

"I know what you mean," said Sean. "It was special for him to visit Megan at Christmas and help Shannon's career."

"He's a good man and a practicing Catholic," said George.

"Maybe so," said Sean. "But right now, he's more of a good solider than a good Catholic, a good soldier following orders that'll result in something terrible to our cause."

"I think he tried to stop things with his trip to Washington," George replied. "I know he got a lot of information from your wife that he took to Washington with him. I think he pleaded the case before the admiral to keep the base open. Maybe he pleaded a good case, but the bomb last month was the final straw. The Protestants force the base closing, and the Protestants take over the base."

"Maybe he tried to stop things," said Sean. "And maybe he pleaded a good case to the admiral. But I don't think there was any possibility of changing the original plans to turn the base over to the Brits. Things were set in stone from the very beginning, and there was nothing he could do to change things."

The two men stopped in front of Sean Kelly's flat.

"Still," said George, "I have mixed emotions about blowing up the base. It puts a bad footnote to one of the best years on the base that I can remember. Captain McKeown's men heavily guard the base. There could be bloodshed."

"There's no other way," said Sean Kelly. "The bad footnote of the whole thing is the Brits taking over the base."

Chapter 27

Army Navy Plan

On August 30, 1977, Jimmy Carter became the first president to speak on the issue of Northern Ireland. The statement of US policy in Northern Ireland was worded carefully and was more significant for its existence than for what it said.

The speech was printed in all the newspapers in Northern Ireland and discussed over pints in pubs. As Carter said, "Throughout our history, Americans have rightly recalled the contributions men and women from many countries have made to the development of the United States. Among the greatest contributions have been those of the British and Irish people, Protestant and Catholic alike. We have close ties of friendship with both parts of Ireland and with Great Britain."

Carter observed that Americans "are deeply concerned about the continuing conflict and violence in Northern Ireland" and know "the overwhelming majority of the people there reject the bomb and the bullet." He said the United States "wholeheartedly supports peaceful means for finding a just solution that involves both parts of the community of Northern Ireland and protects human rights and guarantees freedom from discrimination."

The speech went on for a few more pages but didn't say much more than this. Carter hoped that those engaged in violence would "renounce this course and commit themselves to peaceful pursuit of legitimate goals," but he offered no real policy toward the problems.

George told me, "If the Americans really understood the situation, they would understand that the Catholics of Northern Ireland are just like the American colonies. Both wanted freedom from England."

I found myself in agreement with George O'Donnell. It was becoming easier to understand and feel the position of Catholics in Northern Ireland. The moment in front of the Free Derry wall was something I could not forget. A little girl named Megan in a wheelchair was an image I could not get out of my mind.

꿍

Admiral Schmidt called one day in early September and told me that General Rutledge would be in charge of the handover of the base to the British Army. The general was in command of the British Army in Northern Ireland.

"You'll soon be receiving classified orders," said Admiral Schmidt, "from the Office of the Secretary of Defense and the Chief of Naval Operations to contact General Rutledge. At the same time, the British

Defense Ministry will order the general to contact you to set a date and time for the transfer of all US naval facilities at Londonderry to the British Army."

"We're ready," I said.

"No need to wait for all the official stuff," the admiral said. "I've known Harold Rutledge for years. Just give him a call and arrange to get together to set a time for the handover."

I called General Rutledge and discovered we both had a common interest in golf. The general suggested we set up a golf game at the famous Portrush Golf Club on the north coast of Northern Ireland, not too far from Londonderry. I enthusiastically agreed. I had heard of this legendary course for many years and had dreamed of playing it.

A few days later, I dug out a hunter-green shirt and some khaki pants from one of the temporary storage boxes in the office at Roscommon and drove the thirty miles northeast from Londonderry to the little seaside resort town of Portrush. The town was known for its sandy beaches and the beautiful golf club located on a hill overlooking those beaches.

Like St. Andrews in Scotland, Royal Portrush Golf Club was the first club outside mainland United Kingdom to host the Open Championship in 1951. It was a true links course, overlooking the dark-blue sparkling waters of the North Atlantic. A slight breeze was in the air, and you could smell the sweet odor of turf mixed with a salty sea breeze from the ocean. The dark-green rolling hills of the club were spectacular against the backdrop of blue sky and ocean.

General Rutledge was a portly man somewhere in his seventies. He was wearing his orange plus-fours with a scotch plaid flat hat and waiting at the starter shack with two caddies, ready to hit the links.

The general made small talk during our game.

"You know my troops and I are not the most popular folks in Londonderry," he said.

I smiled. That was the understatement of the year.

"There's not much going on at the base," I replied. "Working things down to a skeleton crew. I'm living at Roscommon, and I have one phone line there and one at the base."

The general was a decent golfer, and it was an even match until the eighteenth when I sank my ball from the sand trap and won the match by two strokes.

After the round of golf, we went into the clubhouse, which required sports jackets as protocol. Neither of us had brought jackets, and we had to borrow a couple that didn't fit quite so well. The general looked funny wearing a jacket with the club logo on it; he was busting out of it with sleeves ending four inches up his wrists. He put down an empty glass of Bushmills Irish whiskey and ordered another.

"My boys are ready to move onto the base," General Rutledge said.

"We're ready for you. We need to move fast. The IRA is planning something soon."

"Seven days from today on Sunday," General Rutledge said. "Full moon out. We move in at three in the morning."

"Good. I'll make sure we're ready."

We both stood up and clinked glasses, and I gave the general a salute as we parted.

Chapter 28

The IRA Plot

At Portrush, while the general and I were planning a time and date for the takeover, a member of the PIRA (Provisional Irish Republican Army), often called just IRA, was also at the club and overheard our conversation. He immediately informed Sean Kelly of the details he heard of the army takeover plan for next Sunday.

The day after my meeting with General Rutledge, Sean Kelly was seen driving a dark-green van through the streets of Londonderry. Next to him in the front seat were two other members of the IRA. The van made stops at various shops and flats around town, picking up other IRA members.

After a few hours, the back of the van was full of boxes with things like "Vinegar" and "Potatoes" written on the outside in an attempt to disguise the sticks of dynamite inside.

In the early evening, the green van stopped at the little pub in the Bogside area of Londonderry that served as one of the meeting places for the IRA. The boxes were unloaded from the van and carried into a room in the rear of the pub, where a large group of IRA members were assembled. They wore black outfits and had heavy belts of ammunition thrown over their shoulders. M16s and all sorts of pistols were everywhere.

George O'Donnell was the only one in the room not dressed in combat gear. He was too old for this kind of thing.

For the next hour, everyone worked stringing the sticks of dynamite together and working out their plan of attack. A large map of the base was spread out on a table in the middle of the room under a bare light bulb.

Sean was always the master strategist for big operations like this one. He picked various men in the room and assigned them to groups. He told everyone to coordinate their watches. Timing was critical.

"This is not going to be a walk in the park, lads," Sean said. "The Yanks are combat veterans with orders to protect the base at all costs."

"Everything is all set," George O'Donnell said. "We need to lower the base to ashes before the British Army takes over. I have warned Captain McKeown about this multiple times."

"We move out from here at one," said Sean. "The other vehicles will be here at twelve thirty. Need everyone back here at twelve tonight. We then drive from here to the Broomhill Hotel and meet there at quarter to one. We take the explosives onto the base at three."

A little before twelve, Jimmy and I walked across the base, perhaps for the last time. The security was tight, and Jimmy could see his men stationed with their M16s all along the perimeter fencing of the base.

We stopped for a moment, as we heard a vehicle pull up outside the fence near the gymnasium. I turned to Jimmy and said, "Let's go see what the hell is going on with that van."

As we headed toward the fence, Jimmy called for support from his armed men.

From the green van outside the gate, George O'Donnell noticed Jimmy and me approaching the fence. He ordered the driver to let him out and then move the van down the road out of sight. "I don't want the captain to get hurt."

The gang looked puzzled and drove away. George showed his ID and proceeded through the main gate, looking for Jimmy and me.

Jimmy and I turned and walked past Sampson Hall. It symbolized for me so much of the life on the base this past year—the dances we had, the commissioning ceremony, and the Christmas party. More than anything else, it seemed to be a symbol of the new spirit and community of the base that had grown so much in the months after the Christmas party. It seemed to represent the promise, the hope I had for the base. The office was closed, and its windows were boarded. All of the files were emptied and transferred to the base in Thurso. Most of the furniture inside had been sold to various businesses in

Londonderry. The mayor had helped by offering businesses that might be interested.

The Enlisted sailor's club and the officer's club were dark. I heard that Carl Campbell got a job as a bartender at a pub in town where his stories of the base would live on, over Guinness and Jameson's.

That mess hall was dark, and most of its cooking implements shipped to Thurso a week before. A few lights were on in the barracks, where the skeleton crew was sleeping until the base closure.

We walked the few blocks over to my home, and I stood in front of it with Jimmy, like he stood in front of Sampson Hall, just looking at it and not saying a word. It had been a good year for the family, one of the best for them. Could it be duplicated in Thurso? Would the marriage last much longer?

Around one, we walked up to the communications center. It was the only place that was still in operation. Since Thurso was not fully operational, Londonderry was still the major communications center for naval forces in the North Atlantic. I walked into the communications center and observed my boys with their headphones on, listening for all of those ships far out on the sea and the submarines under the sea. As I passed a few of the guys, I gave them a pat on the shoulder. They had done such a good job of keeping up the long tradition of the base as the key communications base for the navy in Europe all these years.

When we left the communications center, we walked up to the field where the big radio receivers were located. A slight breeze pushed over the field, riffling the grass and making a strange sound as it went through the big radio towers. It sounded like the transmissions they were receiving. A large moon sat on top of one of the towers, throwing a pale, silver effervescence over the base and almost giving it transcendence like it was briefly taken out of time. Like a vision, we were amazed to see the magnificent aurora borealis; it brought tears to our eyes, as it seemed to be a special send-off.

George could not find us and was just about ready to leave the base when he saw two figures walking down the road that led up to the big receiver towers. He hurried toward the two figures and realized it was Jimmy and me.

"There's not much time," he frantically said. "They're coming tonight!"

"Coming?" I questioned.

"The IRA," George said. "To blow the base sky high."

"Jesus! How the hell do you know this?"

"Just trust me; my sources are never wrong. You must inform the general that the IRA is scheduled to blow up the base at 3:00 a.m. My sources tell me that General Rutledge is staying at the Beech Hill Country House."

I turned and shouted to Jimmy, "Go get your jeep; we are going to Beech Hill Country House."

The country house was only a few miles from the base. The hotel dated from 1729 and was full of antiques and marble fireplaces with bedrooms that had four-poster beds with frilly floral covers.

Jimmy's jeep pulled up the long driveway to the elegant old white hotel, and I jumped out and ran into the hotel.

"I'm Captain McKeown from the American navy base in Londonderry," I said to a dour-looking man at the front desk of the hotel. "I need to talk to General Rutledge immediately."

The deskman could not be hurried for anything. He examined me and then slowly went to a phone and dialed a number.

"General Rutledge is not in his room," he said. "Would you like to leave a message for him?"

"Is there somewhere else in the hotel he might be?"

The man at the front desk motioned to the side.

"You might try the Ardmore restaurant at the hotel."

I ran toward the restaurant. A few people were finishing dinner in the dim light of the old room, but I could not see General Rutledge. I walked around the room, looking for the general, but he was nowhere to be found.

I was ready to leave the restaurant when I heard the familiar British accent of General Rutledge coming from a table in a dark corner. I ran over to the general, who was surprised to see me.

"It's on for tonight," I told General Rutledge. "The IRA is moving onto the base, and they've got enough dynamite to level everything."

General Rutledge got up with the big white starched napkin of the Ardmore still around his neck.

"I need to get to a telephone," he said.

General Rutledge grabbed the phone away from the dour-looking guy at the front desk of the hotel.

"This is General Rutledge!" he yelled into it. "I need to speak with Colonel Montgomery immediately."

The British Command Center was a scattering of tents and tanks set up in a park in downtown Londonderry for the exclusive purpose of carrying out the mission of the base turnover to the British.

Colonel Montgomery listened to General Rutledge on the phone inside one of the tents with increasing concern on his face. When the call was over, Colonel Montgomery sounded the alarm at the command center, and troops came running from all directions.

"Get the tanks up and running!" he yelled. "We're off to the base."

Jimmy and I ran to the jeep and quickly left the hotel; he dropped me off at Roscommon, while he returned to the base and helped gather communication equipment and classified material.

⌁⌁⌁

Meanwhile, Sean Kelly stood in front of the collection of vehicles assembled and watched the British tanks roll past and onto the base. Sean got back into the green van and said to the gang, "It's too late for us to do anything. We'll surely get caught. The turnover is happening now."

In a few minutes, most of the town could feel the vibration of the tanks as they rolled out of the park, down the street, and up the hill to the base.

To their shock, disappointment, and dismay, the British Army began its takeover of the US Navy property in Londonderry. I received a phone call from the temporary gate guard, Petty Officer Martin. He was in a state of panic. "Captain, what shall I do? The British Army tanks are piling onto our base. The British are coming!"

"Tell the remaining crew to gather up any classified material and personal items and proceed to the Roscommon transmitter site. I am on my way. I knew this was coming, so relax and wait for me."

When I arrived at the gate, General Rutledge and Jimmy Emberton were waiting for me. Jimmy reported that our men were running around, gathering up the classified radios, and he had trucks and vans waiting for them.

He had a look of disbelief on his face since I had previously confided in him, but I never disclosed the exact time and date that the British were coming. General Rutledge and I agreed that the American flag would be lowered at 0800 the following morning. I instructed Jimmy to inform our remaining crew that their attendance was required.

I left the base dejected, as a feeling of guilt came over me. I never was able to explain the true reason for closing the base to anyone. Although the closing and transfer of the base was accomplished without injury to any Americans. The people of the town truly loved our sailors. The long and wondrous love affair between the city and the navy was ending.

Chapter 29

The Final Days

At 0800 on September 29, 1977, there was a gathering around the flagpole among a wide circle of British tanks, armored vehicles, British troops, and US naval personnel.

A few of my men circled the flagpole and began singing "The Star-Spangled Banner." The remaining crew joined in. General Rutledge stood at attention off to the side. It would have been a time for the base band to play an off-key rendition of "The Star-Spangled Banner," but the band had been shipped off to Thurso so there was no music for the occasion.

Last view of the American flag

The flag was lowered slowly in customary fashion. Two sailors carefully folded the American flag and gave it to me. A few British troops walked forward, carrying the British Union Jack, and it was raised up the flagpole as the British troops sang "God Save the Queen."

The day after the handover, I packed my suitcase at the office in Roscommon in preparation for my trip on the ferry from Belfast to Scotland. General Rutledge had asked me to play a round of golf at Portrush in celebration of the handover of the base, but I declined the offer. There didn't seem to be anything worth celebrating.

Jimmy drove the navy van, the same van that had taken me and my family from Shannon to Londonderry a little more than a year ago. It seemed like another age, another world altogether.

I asked Jimmy to drive by the base so that we could see it for the last time. We stopped a little before the front gate. The attitude of the new "tenants" was very evident. British troops patrolled the base fence with M16s, and tanks stood inside with their big guns pointed ominously at the world outside the base. Across the entrance that so many visitors had passed through so freely over the last thirty years, there appeared the British Army trademark: barbed wire, rolls and rolls of it.

It was a pleasant day in late September with a cool briskness to it that made you know a new season was approaching. We went through little towns with names like Dungiven, Maghera, Casteldawson, and Toombridge.

Belfast is eighty miles southeast of Londonderry at the bottom of a bay that makes a big dent into the Irish coast. In Belfast, on the way to the ferry docks, we passed a strange, forbidding building on one of the streets.

"I wonder what the hell that is," I asked.

"Orange Hall," Jimmy answered. "Headquarters for the Orangemen in Belfast."

"Ian Nelson's friends. It doesn't surprise me."

Jimmy drove the van into the waiting line for the ferry. There was a little time before the ferry left, so we sat on a pier bench and looked out over the bay in much the way I had looked out at the ocean—looking out to the sea, a familiar thing in the navy. I looked out to the sea and wondered what the world held for me. It was the kind of thing that made navy men. Suddenly, there was a tap on my shoulder from behind. I looked around to see George O'Donnell standing there with a big smile on his face.

"Didn't want to let you get away before saying good-bye," George said.

"I looked for you to say good-bye; you disappeared."

"I couldn't be seen with you and the Brits, Captain."

Then George rolled up his sleeve and revealed a small symbol tattooed on his forearm. It was a green flame encompassing a white lily with an orange stalk.

"What's that?" I asked.

"The Easter lily," said George, "a symbol of remembrance for those who died in the Easter Rising of 1916."

"The IRA?"

George just smiled but did not say anything.

"That's why you knew about the planned attack."

There was a whistle from the ferry.

"She's boarding up now, Captain," said Jimmy.

"Thank you, George," I said, hugging the big man.

"God bless you, Captain. Such a terrible sight to see, the British taking over the base."

"Yes! A terrible sight."

Before he left, George pulled a folded piece of paper out of his pocket and gave it to me. "Reading for your trip to Scotland," he said. "A poem by Joseph Plunkett, who planned the Easter Rising. One of my favorite poems. Something to take with you to Scotland."

Londonderry Farewell

I took the piece of paper and put it into my pocket. Jimmy and I got back into the van and drove onto the ferry. We went up to the top deck. Jimmy headed for the bar and ordered two pints of Guinness. We found a seat near the stern next to the railing. I could see George standing on the dock, waving to us as the ferry pulled away and headed toward Scotland. Jimmy and I took a substantial gulp of Guinness and looked at each other with tears in our eyes.

In half an hour, the ferry was out of the big bay and into the open sea. Ahead, to the east, the outline of the Scottish coast shivered like a mirage in the afternoon sun. And behind, the coast of Ireland sank into the sea.

I reached into my pocket and took out the folded sheet of paper that George had given me. I unfolded it and read the poem by Joseph Plunkett.

I see his blood upon the rose
And in the stars the glory of his eyes,
His body gleams amid eternal snows,
His tears fall from the skies.

I see his face in every flower,
The thunder and the singing of the birds
Are but his voice—and carven by his power
Rocks are his written words.

All pathways by his feet are worn,
His strong heart stirs the ever-beating sea,
His crown of thorns is twined with every thorn,
His cross is every tree.

I looked at the sheet for a few moments. It read, "The reason the IRA did nothing to harm you or your family was because you are an Irish Catholic, and by the way, Father Mullins sends his blessings." I folded the paper and put it back in my pocket. Somewhere down below on the ferry, someone had a radio on and we could hear that song by Andy Gibb, "I Just Want to Be Your Everything." It was a time of disco music back in the States, of wide, white bell-bottom pants, and of celebration in America after the bitter war years of Vietnam, Protestants and Catholics all dancing together.

I wondered whether someday the people in Northern Ireland might find a common God and move toward the vision of Joseph Plunkett and George O'Donnell.

Was it possible to find a peaceful means and just solution that involved both parts of the community of Northern Ireland? Was it possible to find a solution that protected human rights and guaranteed freedom from discrimination? Of course, the people of Northern Ireland were cynical about this and it was almost impossible for them to ever envision this happening.

But I was still young enough to have idealism and hope inside and for a brief moment envisioned a new world of peace. When I thought about this, tears ran down my face and mixed with the salty spray of the sea.

An hour later, the ferry came into the Loch Ryan Bay on the northern tip of Scotland and made its way down to dock in the town of Stranraer. As the ferry pulled in, I could see my family standing on the dock, waving to me—Mary, Colleen, Shawn, and Tara, waving her hobbit.

As I walked off the ferry, I wondered what I should tell Mary—that I was leaving the navy and that we were going back to our little home in Springfield, Virginia, or to some totally new place in the world? I wasn't sure what it was, but I could feel a new life was in front of us.

Mary stood on the dock with hands planted firmly on her hips, while the children tugged at my pants and waist. Mary then came up to me, gave me a kiss, and whispered in my ear, "I hope you plan to retire. Thurso is not my cup of tea, and I hope we are done with separations."

She handed me a sealed envelope from Admiral Schmidt.

I opened it and silently read the message.

"Congratulations on a job well done! No casualties and a perfect turnover to the British Army. It went very smoothly thanks to your leadership and untiring efforts. Our plan is to have you simply spend a year or less getting the base in Thurso going. Your leadership skills in this area are unmatched. When the job is complete, you're being transferred to Honolulu to be the commander of our naval station there, state-of-the-art equipment and a relatively simple job inside the territory of just the good old United States, where Protestants and Catholics go to different churches on Sundays and do not shoot at each other on the other days."

After reading the message, I turned to Mary. "Would you like to go to Hawaii, or would you like me to retire?"

She looked at me in utter shock and said, "Hawaii? Hawaii?"

"Yes, darling! Get out your grass skirt. My next assignment is to take command of a naval base in Hawaii."

Mary reached for me with wide open arms. She was happy, and our marriage had survived. A tear ran down her face. I put my arms around her and pulled her close to me. We laughed and cried together.

Londonderry or Derry~Londonderry Today

The old 6th century walled city of Londonderry, is now the center of culture and creativity. The walls, dating from the 17th century, are still complete, measure one mile in circumference, and stand six meters thick. There are several interesting museums, like the Tower Museum, that tells the history of the city from prehistoric times until today. From here you can take a day trip to the *Giants Causeway*, situated about an hour away on the North Coast, a volcanic formation of thousands of hexagon rocks,

Londonderry is also known for its wild Atlantic coast. Its famous siege Derry~Londonderry, as it is referred to today, is Ireland's only surviving walled city. But don't think for a second that these walls keep you away from experiencing an amazingly beautiful place. Today Northern Ireland's second largest city is a buzzing metropolis with great pubs, fantastic restaurants, and a lively cultural and arts scene.

Wander the bustling streets or cross the stunning Peace Bridge and you'll sense energy in the air. This is a place where things happen, Whether it's the Clipper Yacht Race sweeping into the Foyle Marina, a huge Halloween carnival on the banks of the Foyle, or any number of concerts, plays and exhibitions in the city's impressive selection of many venues and art galleries.

However, there is also Londonderry County, which offers several ways of travel. Rail is very convenient, or for a swift change of pace, you and your friends could be on bikes, following the Foyle Valley Cycle Route to the border towns of Lifford and Strabane. What about a visit to Ness Country Park to check out the highest waterfall in Northern Ireland? Or a thrilling adventure in the Jungle outdoor adventure centre?

Londonderry County has always been famous for its music. The county and city have produced two Nobel Prize winners, Seamus Haney and John Hume, which incidentally, is also the hometown of Choice Music Prize winner SOAK, former Girls Aloud Star Nadine Coyle, and its composer Phil Coulter.

As Phil Coulter put it: "There was music there in the Derry air in the town I loved so well". A heart wrenching tune in which the famous singer laments the tragic history of the "troubles". But he looks forward to a "bright, brand new day" in the future.

***Well there is no doubt the "bright, brand new day" is surely here** in Derry-Londonderry today.*

Source: Northern Ireland Tourism

"The Town I Loved So Well"
Phil Coulter

In my memory, I will always see
The town that I have loved so well
Where our school played ball by the gas yard wall
And they laughed through the smoke and the smell
Going home in the rain, running up the dark lane
Past the jail, and down behind the Fountain
Those were happy days in so many, many ways
In the town I loved so well

In the early morning, the shirt factory horn
Called women from Creggan, the moor, and the bog
While the men on the dole played a mother's role
Fed the children and then walked the dog
And when times got tough there was just about enough

And they saw it through without complaining
For deep inside was a burning pride
In the town I loved so well

There was music there in the Derry air
Like a language that we all could understand
I remember the day that I earned my first pay
When I played in a small pickup band
There I spent my youth, and to tell you the truth
I was sad to leave it all behind me
For I learned about life, and I found a wife
In the town I loved so well

But when I returned, how my eyes have burned
To see how a town could be brought to its knees
By the armored cars and the bombed-out bars
And the gas that hangs on to every breeze
Now the army's installed by that old gas yard wall
And the damned barbed wire gets higher and higher
With their tanks and their guns, oh my god, what have they done
To the town I loved so well

Now the music's gone but they carry on
For their spirit's been bruised, never broken
They will not forget but their hearts are set
On tomorrow and peace once again

Londonderry Farewell

For what's done is done and what's won is won
And what's lost is lost and gone for ever
I can only pray for a bright, brand-new day
In the town I love so well

Appendix B

Relevant Historical Background 1943–1973

1. The Beginnings

Winston Churchill once said that the only thing that frightened him during World War II was the Battle of the Atlantic. The reason was that it provided the supply line for American supplies to England and the other nations fighting Germany. Keeping the pipeline open was essential to defeating Germany.

The most important city in keeping the pipeline open was Londonderry, the furthest northern city in Ireland and strategically located on the River Foyle only four miles from the deep waters of the ocean. During the war, the city took on the mammoth task of supporting the naval ships and crews from over a dozen nations as they escorted the merchant ships and their valuable cargoes across the North Atlantic. These escorts consisted principally of destroyers and lesser craft of the US, Canadian, and British navies.

It all started in April 1941 when arrangements were made with the British government to construct four naval bases in Northern Ireland and Scotland—at Londonderry and Lough Erne in Northern Ireland and Rosneath and Loch Ryan in Scotland. Funds for the construction of these bases were provided by both the British and American governments in accordance with Lend-Lease agreements reached in March 1941. Londonderry and Rosneath provided repair and fueling facilities for destroyers and submarines, ammunition storage, hospitals, and barracks for shore-based personnel. Lough Erne and Loch Ryan were used principally as operations centers for seaplane squadrons.

⌐᷅

Londonderry became home to 20,000 Royal Navy personnel; 10,000 Canadians and Newfoundlanders; and more than 6,000 Americans, as well as men from many of the occupied nations and the soldiers and airmen defending the city and surrounding area. At any one time, there were as many as 140 naval ships and over 30,000 sailors in the port.

With the advent of war, Londonderry immediately became a port of inestimable value as a base for North Atlantic convoy escorts. Its location on the northern coast of Ireland made it the most strategic port for the allocation of supplies to other projects.

The essential North Atlantic sea-lane had its terminus in ports bordering Northern Ireland. As the maintenance of this thin supply line through the ever-tightening German blockade was imperative to the continuance of British resistance, the top priority was given to the project of establishing at Londonderry the first US naval base in the United Kingdom.

⌒⁊⟆⟋

US naval communications in Northern Ireland began out of necessity when the US Naval Operating Base (NOB) at Londonderry became a center of military activity at the beginning of World War II. Allied communications centered around a radio facility that was established as an integral part of the NOB on February 3, 1942. In 1943, the US Navy acquired use of the land upon which the Clooney and Rossdowney compounds were later situated.

The US Naval Radio Station (NAVRADSTA), Londonderry, was established as a separate activity from the US naval operating base (NOB) on July 10, 1944. Thus, this date is considered the actual commencement date of NAVCOMMSTA Londonderry. One month later, on August 15, 1944, the US naval operating base (NOB) was decommissioned, leaving the NAVRADSTA, and its sailors, as the only remaining US Navy activity in Londonderry.

On November 7, 1950, the NAVRADSTA at Londonderry was redesignated as a US naval radio facility (NAVRADFAC). It was later designated a US naval communications station (NAVCOMMSTA) on July 10, 1961.

In the late 1960s, political problems in Northern Ireland began to heat up. On January 30, 1972, thirteen people were killed (seven teenagers) in Londonderry as a result of the battle between the Provisional IRA and the government of Northern Ireland. The event was known as "Bloody Sunday" and marked the beginning of the period of intense fighting between the Catholics and Protestants in Northern Ireland called the "troubles." The US naval communications station was situated in the middle of the conflict.

Because of the danger to American lives in Londonderry, there began a series of communications between the American embassy in London and the US State Department in Washington, DC. The communications were classified for many years and were recently declassified.

2. Fear of Violence
Declassified Communications
1973–1975

DATE: June 1973
FROM: American Consulate Belfast
TO: Secretary of State, Washington, DC, American Embassy Dublin, US NAV COMM STA Londonderry
SUBJECT: Londonderry Base May Become Provo Target

1. Paul Hastings-Caughey, a journalist, told Congen today that Londonderry Provos are in process of deciding that US NAV-COMM STA will be made legitimate target of their operation. Hastings-Caughey presented credentials of "North Atlantic Press" and claims to have done work for the (London) *Times* and to be in N.I. to do story for the *N.Y. Times* on Gerald Brady case. H-C said his source was one Seamus Kelly and identified later as Londonderry Provo leader on the run and living over border in Letterkenny. Congen wondered why Provos would contemplate such action and particularly if reason might be importance of base payroll to economy of community. H-C said that was it. Base commander has been informed of foregoing.

2. To Belfast's knowledge only person who has even halfway seriously mentioned attack on Londonderry base was Mrs. Bernadette McAliskey (Devlin) as she insists now on being

called. Her idea, explained in her "Price of My Soul" (p. 77) was to cause diplomatic incident by blowing up base installations to bring "Northern Ireland to the attention of the world." She of course had said she supports officials (not Provos).

3. Comment: Attacks on Londonderry base would seem highly unlikely. They would be about surest way one could think of to dry up financial support in US for Provos. Hastings-Caughey not known to local *London Times* people.

〜〻〜

DATE: March 1974
FROM: American Embassy London
TO: Secretary of State Washington, DC, American Consulate Belfast, Secretary of Defense
SUBJECT: Raid on NAV COMM STA Londonderry

1. In response to embassy request for assessment, FCO told Emboff March 19 that investigation of unsuccessful raid on NAV COMM STA Armory March 17 was continuing. It is thought that a total of 7 people were involved. Police authorities in NI are holding 4 people (2 male, 2 female) on minor charges pending development of further evidence. All 4 are identified as Provisional IRA.

2. Preliminary British assessment is that raid was probably a free-lance operation unauthorized by IRA command. They note that raid was very ineptly executed. Confidential British do not believe that raid suggests that IRA have changed previous policy of avoiding attacks on US installations.

～スミ～

DATE: April 1975
FROM: Secretary of State Washington, DC
TO: American Embassy London
SUBJECT: Realignment of Naval Telecommunications System (NTS)

1. New communication technology offers the prospect of con-solidation of communications functions at single sites with considerable financial savings. In consonance with these tech-nical advances, the US Navy is planning to realign the NTS in the UK. Preliminary planning envisions closure of the Naval Communications Station Londonderry and attendant NTS facilities in Northern Ireland, with management, sup-port, and operations being relocated to another US Navy com-munications oriented activity in the UK. Two sites currently under consideration are the naval security group activity in Edzell, Scotland, and the Naval Radio Station (Transmitter) at Thurso, Scotland.

2. In view of the strong Congressional interest in reducing the support manpower in Europe, emphasis being placed on realignment in that area, while it appears that additional land will not be required beyond that already available at Edzell and Thurso, it is anticipated that some construction, such as expansion of current facilities and antenna additions, will be required. The target date for completion is FY 1977.

3. Detailed information will be provided when the specific site has been selected in order that formal consultations can be undertaken with the British government. In the meantime, it is desirable that we discuss this informally with the British government to preclude embarrassment should such planning come to their attention prematurely. It is requested that department be notified when such discussions have been completed with any reaction.

⌒⟋⟍⌒

DATE: April 1975
FROM: American Embassy London
TO: Secretary of State, Washington, DC
SUBJECT: Realignment of Naval Telecommunications System (NTS)

1. We raised subject of realignment of NTS with assistant head of FCO North America Department, Neil Smith, and US Desk

Officer Graham Archer on April 8. We stressed that this was informal advice that US is considering plan to realign NTS and that we would seek HMG approval when we have a detailed proposal.

2. Initial reaction of FCO officials was that plan is understandable in terms of technical parameters and in context of reduction of support manpower in Europe. They could foresee, however, that plan might cause problems for Northern Ireland office and Scottish office. Former would be troubled by fact that important source of employment in Northern Ireland would be removed with consequent economic problem for Londonderry area. Scottish office might well be troubled by any noticeable construction at Thurso or Edzell, such as large antenna that might "further detract from the natural beauty of the area." (Comment: Archer, who made above comment, has been closely associated with discussions of possible USN construction at Holy Loch and has in mind the strong position taken by the Scottish office against activities that would injure beauty of rural areas of Scotland.

3. Specific questions asked were (A) how many more people will be stationed in Scotland and (B) what will be physical nature of construction at Scottish site. Even though US plan is not complete, it would be useful if we could give an interim reply to above questions.

～⁊⫯⋋～

DATE: July 1975

FROM: Secretary of State, Washington, DC

TO: American Embassy London

SUBJECT: Realignment of Naval Telecommunications System (NTS)

1. Preliminary planning referenced in State 77246 now complete. Navy proposes to relocate all communications management, support, and operations from NAV COMM STA Londonderry to Naval Radio Station, Thurso, Scotland, which would then be known as NAV COMM STA UK. Target date for the activation of NAV COMM STA UK is July 1977.

2. The proposal is based on survey confirming that Thurso provides most economical site with most efficient management of existing buildings to accommodate relocated functions. The present mess hall can handle the planned expansion, and some housing is available on base for married and unmarried personnel. This relocation plan offers significant advantages through collocation of communications stations functions with a transmitter site (FORSS), which is located in close proximity with receiver site (West Murkle). The following basic elements of the plan answer questions posed in Reftel A.

3. In Northern Ireland, manpower would be reduced from the present level of 18 officers, 280 enlisted, and 107 local nationals to zero by December 1977. All land under the management of NAV COMM STA Londonderry would be returned to the host government. Closure would follow activation of NAV COMM STA UK by approximately three to six months.

4. New construction in Scotland would include a forty-foot parabolic antenna protected by a dome and housing for associated satellite earth terminal equipment on the existing receiver site at West Murkle, some additional antennas at the existing antenna fields, and additional housing for personnel in the event that adequate private rental is not available. Manpower would be increased at Thurso by about 3 officers, 119 enlisted men, and 4 local national civilians. The expected increase in demand for housing in the Thurso area would be approximately 76 units, including a mix of apartments, private rooms, and houses.

5. Request you obtain HMG approval for the proposed realignment of communications facilities. Even though the planned consolidation would not be completed until two years from now, such approval would permit timely notification of the civilian personnel affected and facilitate an orderly transition.

～⌒⋁⌒～

DATE: September 1975
FROM: American Embassy London
TO: Secretary of State, Washington, DC
SUBJECT: Realignment of Naval Telecommunications System (NTS)

1. Defense Department, FCO, has now replied in an 18 September letter to our 17 July letter requesting HMG's approval "as soon as possible" for the Londonderry to Thurso relocation.

"You wrote to Teddy Jackson on 17 July about the transfer of US Naval Communications facilities from Londonderry to Thurso in Scotland. When we discussed this recently I said that we would be sending you a standard form of questionnaire, which has to be completed whenever a proposal is made for the modification of communications facilities in the UK. I now enclose a copy of the questionnaire, and would be grateful if it could be completed and returned in due course. We should also be grateful if, in order to enable us to consider all the implications of the move, you could let us know (A) what restrictions there are at present on the use of the surrounding land as a result of the existing installation at West Murkle and (B) what additional restrictions would be imposed as a result of the new development. For instance, will the US Navy want to prohibit certain developments or activities within a given radius of the station? (With other communications stations it has sometimes been necessary to prohibit such processes as arc-welding within a certain radius and also to limit the use of other electrical equipment). We need this information in order to know to what extent additional land in an area which is keen to accept industrial development would be sterilized by the relocation of these facilities at Thurso."

2. We have passed to CINCUSNAVEUR the questionnaire and letter.

DATE: October 1975

FROM: American Embassy London

TO: Secretary of State, Washington, DC

SUBJECT: Expansion of Belfast/London HF Radio Network

1. AMCONSUL Belfast desires expand HF radio net to include Dublin and Londonderry. Radio located residence Consul General. Londonderry link would fit in with E & E plans, which call for division of city for emergency planning purposes with residence being focal point in case of evacuation (See Belfast A-54 September 19, 1975, being pouched Stuttgart for clearance, then to the Department for distribution).

2. Radio contact between London and Belfast made on 4.470 MHZ with unsatisfactory results. Suspect problem caused by location of antenna within the residence attic. Congen proposes have antenna installed nearby trees. This would avoid pinpointing residence with located in housing area occupied by members of Ulster Volunteer Force and Ulster Defense Association.

3. Request advice.

DATE: November 1975
FROM: American Embassy London
TO: Secretary of State, Washington, DC
SUBJECT: Realignment of Naval Telecommunications System

1. We have received from Pellew, Defense Department, FCO, a letter stating that HMG does not anticipate any difficulties arising from the information we supplied them on October 16. They are hopeful that departmental comments on the information we supplied will be cleared by December 8.

2. On the matter of a public announcement, the FCO asks that we give some thought to one "in view of possible public misunderstanding arising from the closure at Londonderry and the expansion at Thurso." It is the FCO's view that such a statement should stress the technical reasons for the closure at Londonderry "thus minimizing any implications of loss of confidence in the security situation." Also, any such statement should make clear that expansion at Thurso will "not disturb the environment or limit the prospects for industrial development in the area." Pellew asks that USG draft a confidential statement and give HMG opportunity to comment on it.

3. We are passing to CINCUSNAVEUR a copy of the site clearance form which the British are circulating for clearance.

DATE: December 1975
FROM: American Embassy London
TO: Secretary of State, Washington, DC
SUBJECT: Realignment of Naval Telecommunications System

1. Ref (A) (Which we understand is available in OSD) contains CINCUSNAVEUR proposed text of public affairs response to inquiries about realignment of Naval Telecommunications Systems involving Londonderry and Thurso.

2. Embassy concurs in draft press release and questions and answers with exception of answer three. We suggest that second sentence be modified to say, "almost two years ago on 10 April 1974." We concur that if asked US should not withhold information on explosion at microwave tower, but we think that this answer should emphasize how long ago it took place in order to demonstrate that this incident was not connected with the decision to confidential realign naval communications in the UK.

3. St. Patrick's Day
March 1976

On St. Patrick's Day in 1976, Prime Minister Cosgrave of Northern Ireland visited the White House. It had a special symbolic significance in that President Ford, for the most part, had ignored the Northern Ireland issues during his term in office in his attempts to focus on domestic issues. As leading Irish scholar Joseph Thompson writes in *American Policy and Northern Ireland: A Saga of Peace Building*, Ford's "heroic efforts to bring the United States to domestic political normalcy allowed Kissinger and the State Department to continue to reject America's moral crusades."

However, as Thompson observes, the question still remained whether international outcries of human rights violations were a valid issue for the US government policy of realpolitik. Members of Congress believed that a humanitarian foreign policy was preferable to realpolitik, and so they began to develop links with nationalist and republican leaders in Northern Ireland. But the moral vacuum in American government policy toward Northern Ireland would not be filled until the presidency of Jimmy Carter.

The White House dinner for Cosgrove in 1976 was lighthearted and celebratory of the close Irish-American friendship. President Ford told the Irish prime minister, "Betty and I had the luck of the Americans to have you with us tonight. On this St. Patrick's Day of the US Bicentennial Year, all Americans know there is a bit of the green in the red, white, and blue of the United States. We honor the history of our nation and the great contributions that all of you from

Ireland have made to American independence, as well as growth. No country could be more welcome or entitled to join our bicentennial celebration than Ireland."

While the dinner was lighthearted and celebratory, Ford and Cosgrove did discuss the violence in Northern Ireland privately. A summary of their meeting in the *American Presidency Project* entered on March 18, 1976, observed, "The President and the Prime Minister noted with regret the continued violence arising from the Northern Ireland situation. They deplored all support for organizations involved directly or indirectly in campaigns of violence and reiterated in particular their determination to continue and to intensify their cooperation in the prosecution of illegal activities. They appealed to the American and Irish people to refrain from supporting, with financial or other aid, this violence.

〜⁊⫯〜

A few hundred miles north of Washington, in New York City, presidential candidate Jimmy Carter marched in the St. Patrick's Day parade down Fifth Avenue, wearing a button that said, "England get out of Ireland."

During Carter's election campaign of 1976, the former governor of Georgia had become involved in the ongoing issue of Northern Ireland. There is evidence from British documents of the time of British concern that the potential election of the first Democratic president since the onset of the Northern Ireland troubles would see the United States take a more active role under the direction of the influential Irish-American lobby. Reports emerged that Senator Daniel Patrick Moynihan had even pressed for the inclusion of a section on Northern Ireland in the Democratic Party platform, although this never materialized. But a different American relationship to Northern Ireland was in the air.

About the Authors

Thomas McKeown
USN (Ret), CAPT

Captain McKeown has a BS in mathematics from Seton Hall University and an MS in telecommunications engineering from the US Naval Postgraduate School. He has also done graduate work at the Harvard Business School in corporate strategic planning and advanced marketing management. He has had a distinguished career in the military as well as civilian life. He is a highly decorated navy officer, whose career has included two Meritorious Service medals, one during combat duty as CO of the naval telecommunications base in Vietnam. His naval service included four telecommunications commands as well as command of two surface warfare ships. His civilian career has included work for a number of well-known corporations as well as for the government and educational institutions, including doing strategic planning for the US Treasury Department and for W. Paul Stillman School of Business at Seton Hall University and acting as executive program director for Gartner Research Corporation. His most recent strategic planning project was for the city of Washington, DC. He lives in Palm Desert, California.

John Fraim

John has a BA from UCLA and a JD from Loyola Law School. He is president of GreatHouse Marketing Strategy, a marketing consulting firm, and GreatHouse Stories in Palm Desert, California, which assists clients in writing biographies, histories, and memoirs. John has been a writer all his life with numerous published works and three published books. One of his books is the award-winning *Spirit Catcher*, the life and art of legendary jazz musician John Coltrane, which earned the best biography award from the Small Press Association. He is involved in a number of community activities and is a member of the Palm Springs Writers Guild board of directors. A recognized expert on symbolism, he is the author of *Battle of Symbols* and served as a consultant on the film *The Da Vinci Code*. He writes a regular column for *Script* magazine, the largest publication for screenwriters. He is currently at work on a history of Palm Desert as well as a biography of a world-renowned nutritionist and a famous paleontologist.

57410816R00140

Made in the USA
Columbia, SC
08 May 2019